Civil Rights.
A Quick Immersion

Quick Immersions provide illuminating introductions to diverse topics in the worlds of social science, the hard sciences, philosophy and the humanities. Written in clear and straightforward language by prestigious authors, the texts also offer valuable insights to readers seeking a deeper knowledge of those fields.

Andrew Altman

CIVIL RIGHTS
A Quick Immersion

Tibidabo Publishing
New York

Published by Tibidabo Publishing, Inc. New York.

Copyediting by Lori Gerson
Cover art by Raimon Guirado

First published 2021

Visit our Series on our Web:
www.quickimmersions.com

ISBN: 978-1-949845-23-5
1 2 3 4 5 6 7 8 9 10

Library of Congress Control Number: 2020949795

Printed in the United States of America.

Contents

List of illustrations

Introduction

The idea of civil rights has played a central role in the political history of the world over the past several centuries. Alongside the concepts of natural rights and human rights, the idea has animated the actions of countless persons and groups aiming to transform their own societies and even the global order. But what are civil rights? Which rights count as civil rights? How do civil rights differ from natural and human rights? Why did the idea of civil rights play such an important role in the history of the modern era? And is the idea a valuable one for addressing key issues in the early decades of the 21st century?

There is a simple and quick answer to the question of what civil rights are. They are the rights to which every citizen of a modern state is morally entitled. But the meaning of that answer can barely be understood without some grasp of the answers to the other questions posed in the previous paragraph. This book is devoted to answering those questions. Along the way, additional matters must be addressed, such as: What is a modern state? What is citizenship? How did citizenship under pre-modern political arrangements differ from modern citizenship?

The approach of this book is both historical and philosophical. The book explains the idea of civil rights by looking at its use over the centuries in major legal and political controversies over who gets to be a full member of society and what that membership entails. The explanation aims to develop a philosophically illuminating account of the idea, drawing connections between it and concepts that many modern political philosophers have carefully studied, such as the concepts of natural and human rights, individual freedom, national self-determination, discrimination, and democracy.

Civil rights movements are organized and persistent legal and political battles by some substantial proportion of the members of subordinated social groups seeking to achieve the full rights of citizenship. Three historic civil rights movements receive considerable attention in this book: the Civil Rights Movement of Black Americans, the emancipation of European Jews, and the women's movements of the 19th and 20th centuries. Understanding how these struggles for civil rights proceeded, and the respects in which they succeeded or failed, helps us to grasp the idea of civil rights as it has played out in the lives of people who have been denied equal citizenship.

Among the ideological rationalizations that the privileged members of society have regularly used to deny equality to others is the notion that the members of subordinated groups are content with their condition. The most extreme version of this argument was found among the defenders of slavery, but it was also put forth by those seeking to justify the Jim Crow system of racial subjugation as well as the patriarchal subordination of women. The most effective practical refutations of this kind of supremacist rationalization are the various acts of resistance and rebellion undertaken by the subordinated. If conditions permit the subordinated to engage in organized mass action against their condition, so much the better. And civil rights movements as a form of such action have represented a compelling practical negation of a key piece of supremacist ideology.

The efforts of subordinated segments of society to gain civil rights are aptly characterized as "struggles," because there is invariably strong opposition to the extension of those rights, and, without concerted and sustained pressure on the power centers of society, the efforts would be doomed to total defeat. Frederick Douglass made the point emphatically: "If there is no struggle there is no progress. Those who profess to favor freedom and yet deprecate agitation are men who want crops without plowing up the ground ... Power concedes nothing without a demand. It never did and it never will" (1857).

The modern idea of civil rights was born in the French Revolution, with its idea that citizens of a republic possessed a status that subjects of an absolute monarch lacked. That status was defined by the possession of civil rights. A monarch might grant certain advantages or favors to some or all subjects, but the grant was revocable at the will of the monarch. Civil rights were thought to be claims that were not subject to legitimate revocation by any authority.

In a crucial sense, then, the rights with which we are concerned in this book cannot be granted or revoked, but they can be recognized, protected, or violated. In this sense, civil rights are moral rights, i.e., legitimate moral claims that the individual can make against others, including against any ruling powers that might stand over him. Such claims can be ignored or violated, but doing so does not weaken their validity as claims. Civil rights are, in one sense, then, valid moral claims that persons can make, regardless of whether or not those claims are recognized and respected by others. The struggle for civil rights, in this sense, is a fight for the recognition and protection of those claims by society and its government. In this sense, to talk of civil rights is not to make descriptive statements about how government actually treats its citizens but rather to put forth prescriptive claims about how citizens ought to be treated by their government.

In a second sense of 'civil rights', we can speak of a ruler or government granting or rescinding such rights. We mean that a government is recognizing and undertaking to protect the valid moral claims that constitute civil rights in the previous sense, or that the government is taking back that recognition or undertaking. In this sense, to talk of the civil rights that citizens have is to make descriptive statements about what a government is in fact doing.

When civil rights are thought of as legal rights that persons have, it is the second sense that is the appropriate one. Legal rights can be granted, and when they are so, then persons actually possess them, at least "on paper." Legal rights can be violated as well, but the point is that, when a legal claim is violated, it must have been granted by the government or otherwise posited by society (as in customary law) in the first place. Civil rights as valid moral claims —the first sense— do not need to have been previously posited and can be violated even when they have not been recognized by the law. And when we think of civil rights as legal rights that persons ought to have, even though they do not at present possess them, it is the first sense that is the appropriate one: the thought is that the law ought to recognize and protect certain valid moral claims.

Although the core meaning of the idea of civil rights denotes the rights to which citizens of a modern society are morally entitled, it does not follow that persons who are not citizens of the country in which they live lack all such rights. Many civil rights are also human rights, possessed by individuals in virtue of their being human, regardless of their citizenship status. The rights against being enslaved, tortured or subjected to arbitrary arrest and imprisonment are all civil rights that are also human rights. Moreover, some residents of a country who lack a legal right to citizenship might, nonetheless, be morally entitled to become citizens. As we will see in Chapter Four, shortly before the American Civil War, the U.S. Supreme Court infamously declared that persons of African ancestry were not, and could never become, citizens of the nation. The court's declaration was an egregious violation of the moral rights of American Blacks. So civil rights, in the moral sense, belong not only to persons who are recognized by law as citizens but also to those who have a right to be so recognized.

A subset of civil rights is often referred to as 'civil liberties'. The latter term encompasses freedom of conscience and expression, freedom of the press, the rights to private property, privacy and due process of law, and the right to vote. There is disagreement over whether or not rights against discrimination are civil liberties. But the standard use of the term over the past century has deliberately excluded rights to economic resources such as health care, a job, and a minimum income. By contrast, many thinkers and activists have argued that such economic rights are civil rights, and their view has been accepted in much of the world. However, as I note in the Postscript, the view is under increasing pressure from the ideological and economic forces of neoliberal capitalism, and the future of the view is uncertain.

Chapter 1
Key Concepts

I. Moral Rights

The idea of moral rights has been a crucial part of moral discourse since the 17th century, and philosophers have developed various accounts of the idea. In this Chapter, I present some key features of moral rights as they are understood across a range of accounts.

To say that an individual has moral rights is to say that he is owed certain treatment by other individuals and by institutions, so that, whenever he is treated otherwise, he has been wronged. It is not simply that something wrong has been done but that the wrong has been done *to him*. And for that reason, he has a special standing to demand that the wrong cease and that reparations be made to him.

When I say that moral rights entail that an individual is owed certain "treatment," I mean to encompass omissions as well as actions. If I promise you to do something, then, assuming that certain conditions are met (e.g., I am not promising to commit a moral wrong such as murder), then I owe it to you to do what I promised. My failure to do it, even though it is an omission rather than an action, amounts to treating you in a way that violates your right. This point about omissions is relevant in discussions about what governments owe to their citizens. An omission by government, e.g., the failure of American governments at the state and national levels to protect Blacks and their White allies from physical assault when they were peacefully protesting during the Civil Rights Movement, can be a violation of legal and moral rights. Some state and local officials *also* violated the rights of protestors by assaulting them, but the simple failure to protect the protestors amounted to "treatment" that violated rights.

An important feature of many moral rights is that they give decision-making authority to the individual person. For example, the right of religious liberty means that it is up to each person to decide for herself which religion to worship. Others might desire that she follow their creed, but they have no authority to decide the matter for her. Any effort by them to compel her to worship in a particular manner infringes on the decision-making authority that the right of religious liberty confers on her as an individual. Moreover, because the authority to decide is held by the individual, she is in a special position to demand that any infringement on her authority cease: she has a certain moral standing in this respect that others lack, though they can legitimately support her demand.

In the modern world, the moral status accorded to the individual has been captured using the idea of rights. Concepts like the good of society or the greatest happiness for the greatest number do not seem to be adequate for capturing that status. Those concepts look at individuals in the aggregate and give us a way of talking about what is good overall. The idea of rights looks at individuals one-by-one and gives us a way of talking about what each is owed.

Many modern philosophers have claimed that all moral rights are held ultimately by individuals and that groups cannot have rights that are irreducible to the rights of the individual members. I am skeptical of that view, because I think that certain human populations can have an irreducible moral right to rule themselves in the way that they collectively choose. The question of whether or not a collective moral right to political self-determination is a civil right will be examined later (see Chapter Two, section IV). The point to be made here is that, if there is such a collective moral right, then something akin to the moral status of the individual will be held by certain collectivities. Denying those collectivities political self-determination would be a wrong to them, amounting to a refusal to accord them what they are owed, and their claim that the denial cease would carry special moral weight. So although moral rights were initially conceived as belonging exclusively to the individual and the idea of such rights captures well the moral status that modernity has attributed to the individual, we should not automatically dismiss the possibility that some collectivities have certain irreducible moral rights.

II. Privileges and Rights

In one sense, privileges are claims that persons enjoy at the discretion of a ruling power. In this sense, privileges can be extended or rescinded by the arbitrary will of that power. In imperial China, subjects had privileges in this sense, but none had rights. Subjects had no legally or socially-recognized standing to insist that they be treated in a certain way. The Emperor and the imperial bureaucracy exercised unlimited discretion.

In Europe, from medieval times to the end of the 18th century, Jews also had privileges in the same sense but no rights. Europe's ruling Christian powers permitted Jews to reside in assigned places and to pursue designated occupations. But these permissions were at the discretion of the ruling powers and were often in force only for limited periods of time, after which they were withdrawn. Jews had no legally or socially-recognized claim that they be permitted to live where they were born or had resided for years. Thus, the expulsion of Jews from various cities and countries was a feature of European history for centuries. By contrast, under customary law, Christians did have rights of residence: they had a secure claim against being treated like Jews and expelled from the places where they lived.

So in one sense, a privilege is a precarious permission granted at the will of the ruler and subject to being withdrawn at the ruler's discretion. But in another sense, a privilege refers to a special claim that some, but not all, persons living under a given system of political rule can make as a matter of right. In this sense, the Christians of 18th century Europe had many privileges that were denied to Jews, including privileges of residency and occupation. This sense of privilege does not stand in contrast to rights, but rather it is a kind of right that serves to distinguish one part of a population from another. Thus, Christians were privileged in comparison to Jews. Similarly, in some European countries during the early modern era, Roman Catholics were privileged in comparison to Lutherans and Calvinists, and in other countries the reverse situation held. Along the same lines, the system of guilds granted privileges to guild members to pursue a given occupation, a privilege that non-members lacked. Privileges thus established the superior legal status of some persons and the inferior status of others.

III. The Civil-Political Distinction

Civil rights were originally regarded as distinct from political rights. Civil rights included the freedoms to own and inherit property, enter into contracts, bring lawsuits, testify in court, get married, have children, receive an education, reside in and travel to any region of one's country, enter into any lawful occupation, form private associations, and practice one's religion. Political rights included the freedoms to vote and to be elected or appointed to public office.

The civil-political distinction was not a mere conceptual difference that might be entertained by philosophers while it was ignored by everyone else. Rather, the distinction had a crucial implication, for its meaning in practice was that there was no need to extend political rights to female or Black citizens: their citizenship entitled them to (some) civil rights but not to any political rights, which were reserved to other citizens (see Chapter Two, section II). But over the course of the 19th and early 20th centuries, it became increasingly clear that the two sets of rights were more closely linked than had been previously acknowledged. In particular, it was unrealistic to think that people could securely enjoy their civil rights if they lacked political rights. Without the right to vote, women invariably were second-class citizens whose civil rights were unduly restricted and frequently violated. The feminist movements of the late 19th and early 20th centuries typically pushed hard for the franchise only after finding that the lack of the vote was hampering their efforts to gain economic and other rights. And without effective access to the ballot box, America's Blacks found that their civil rights were routinely denied and trampled upon by Whites.

The lesson of history was that, to protect their civil rights, individuals from subordinated groups needed the rights to vote and hold office and that the practical meaning of the civil-political distinction should be repudiated. Even so, the International Covenant on Civil and Political Rights (1966) was given a title that wrongly implied that there was a defensible civil-political distinction. Nonetheless, political rights are today counted among civil rights by any reasonably well-informed person.

IV. Freedom, Equality, and Discrimination

It is a striking fact about the American Civil Rights Movement that its demands and grievances were formulated in the language of freedom much more often than in the language of equality. The political theorist Richard H. King observed, "The rhetoric of freedom permeated the movement from the beginning ... There was surprisingly little talk about equality" (1992: 13- 14). And Martin Luther King, Jr. gave clear voice to the aspirations of those participating in the movement when he said simply, "The Negroes' goal is freedom," (1968: 111) a point that he repeated many times.

There is now a strong tendency to think that the movement was about equality rather than freedom. But Blacks at the time said repeatedly to White Americans, "We demand freedom;" much less frequently did they say, "We demand equality." In a similar vein, the term 'Jewish emancipation' reflects the centrality of freedom in the way that European Jews and their Christian allies thought of the extension of civil rights to Jews. And the women who sought to have their rightful claims recognized and secured often characterized their efforts as seeking emancipation from a kind of slavery. The women's movement of the 1960's was called by its proponents "women's liberation," before reactionaries succeeded in derisively reducing the term to "women's lib." In calling for liberation, women were affirming the continuity of their movement with emancipatory struggles going back to the days of the abolitionists. Similarly, advocates of rights for gays have fought for "gay liberation."

In one sense, 'emancipation' refers to liberation from the bonds of slavery. But there is a broader sense in which the term refers to the freeing of individuals from rigid social roles, identities, and hierarchies that impose unjust disadvantages on them. In light of this broader sense, it is difficult to escape the conclusion that freedom is at the center of virtually all movements for civil rights.

But what about equality? Aren't civil rights about equality as well? Yes. Civil rights movements have aimed at securing equal respect and recognition for the agency and well-being of persons who have had their freedom wrongfully abridged and their well-being wrongfully ignored or discounted on account of the particular group in society to which they belong. Freedom is what enables persons to exercise their agency, i.e., the capacity of each person to decide for himself which ends to pursue. Well-being consists in the satisfaction of a person's interests. The unequal treatment that is the target of civil rights movements constitutes wrongful discrimination that harms the agency and well-being of individuals. The focus on freedom by the various movements was not meant to deny the centrality of equality or well-being. Rather, the members of the subordinated group were underscoring their own agency, manifested in the very act of demanding the freedoms that would protect the exercise of that agency.

Some philosophers have dismissed the idea of equality as misguided. They argue that each person should have his or her rights respected and that what those rights are does not depend on what rights others have. My right to freedom of expression does not depend on your right to freedom of expression, or vice-versa; it depends on my status as an adult human being with ideas and opinions. According to the critics of equality, if government censors me but not you, then it has violated my rights, but not because of the different way in which it has treated us. The idea of equality mistakenly suggests, say the critics, that the wrong committed by government against me lies in the differential treatment.

However, the critics are the ones who are mistaken in their dismissal of equality. Government often has discretion in the way it treats its citizens: there is a range of things it can legitimately do, and it has the rightful authority to choose from the options in that range. If government provides a certain level of benefits to Whites, then it is obligated to provide the same level for Blacks, and the rights of Blacks are violated if a lower level of benefits is provided to them on account of their race.

Consider that government is morally obligated to provide for the education of children. A government might have significant discretion in deciding on how much funding schools should receive. Under Jim Crow, Black schools received much less funding than White schools. Black children were wronged because the level of funding for their schools was below what government had a moral obligation to provide: the children's right to an adequate education was violated. But that is not the end of the matter. There was a second wrong to Blacks: their right not to be discriminated against because of their race was also violated. If southern states had raised funding levels for Black schools to make them adequate, though still not as well-funded as White schools, then the first wrong would be rectified. But the second wrong, the wrong of discrimination, would have been left in place.

V. The Arc of the Moral Universe?

In an 1852 sermon, the abolitionist Unitarian minister Theodore Parker gave voice to the belief that the forces of history were on the side of justice: "Look at the facts of the world. You see a continual and progressive triumph of the right. I do not pretend to understand the moral universe, the arc is a long one, my eye reaches but little ways ... But from what I see I am sure it bends towards justice" (6). More than a century later, during the Civil Rights Movement, Martin Luther King gave Parker's words a concise formulation: "The arc of the moral universe is long, but it bends towards justice" (1986: 230).

Nonetheless, the history of civil rights shows that progress is fragile, fragmentary, and reversible and that the facts of the world provide little grounds for thinking that there is a metaphysical guarantee of progress. No sensible person would doubt that, on the whole, civil rights are better secured now than they were in the worlds of Parker and King. But matters would have looked very different if the judgment were made in light of how things stood in the world in 1941, when Nazi Germany was relentlessly extending its grip across Europe and imperial Japan had subjugated much of East Asia. It takes a leap of faith to think that it was preordained that the Axis powers would not dominate the world for generations and bury the very idea of civil rights.

There is a backward-looking analogue to the forward-looking belief that history is on the side of justice. In the eyes of many people looking back at the phases of history that brought about moral progress, it appears that the progress was inevitable. But the progress we see in history was no more inevitable than is the progress which we hope to see in the future. Perhaps it was psychologically important for abolitionists like Parker to believe in inevitable progress that could not be undone, else they would have been unable to muster the resolve to fight against what seemed to most observers at the time insurmountable odds. And perhaps something similar could be said about King and his struggle against Jim Crow. But looking at matters from a more detached perspective, the success or failure of struggles for justice is a profoundly contingent matter.

Chapter 2
Society, Law, and Politics

I. Modern Society

The idea of civil rights has played a key role in the development of modern life, and it has its appropriate place in the context of the arrangements, institutions, and moral-political consciousness of modern society. It would be anachronistic to talk of civil rights in the context of ancient or medieval societies, which lacked the institutions and understanding of politics and personhood to make sense of the concept of civil rights. Modern society is the home of civil rights. But what is modern society?

Modern societies are generally characterized by 1) a highly differentiated economy, with many sectors and most production taking place outside of the household, 2) a government bureaucracy that applies official decisions and rules, 3) a sizeable middle class, including owners of small-scale businesses and professionals such as lawyers, physicians, and teachers, 4) a system of formal education, 5) a uniform system of laws and courts, and 6) a consciousness of the moral and political importance of individual freedom. Historically, the emergence of such societies from their pre-modern predecessors brought with it a substantial diminution of traditional social and legal constraints on individual freedom. The idea of civil rights was used in thinking about the scope of freedom and the degree of social protection to which individuals were entitled. At the same time, the idea was especially important to those groups of persons —including women, Jews, and Blacks— who were subjected to subordination, even as socially-recognized rights were being extended to other members of their society.

When the denial of civil rights tracks social categories that structure interaction in a given society, systemic injustice thereby arises. In paradigmatic cases, the categories have revolved around social identities relating to race, religion, gender, sexual orientation, and disability, among others. In those cases, the victims tend to be disadvantaged in a relatively comprehensive way: they are denied not just one civil right but a number of them. The reason is straightforward: the denial of rights typically rests on the belief that the members of the social group in question are inferior in important ways to the rest of the population and/or are especially dangerous to others, and claims of group inferiority and danger tend to provide a rationale for the denial of a number of key civil rights to the group's members.

Because civil rights belong to the individual as such, a lone person or a miscellaneous collection of persons can be deprived of their civil rights. The deprivations need not track significant social categories and can be perpetrated for idiosyncratic reasons. Nonetheless, it is not an accident that the most extensive and comprehensive deprivations of civil rights in fact track such categories. Social categories and the identities based on them are linked to social norms that guide the behavior and thinking of the majority of those who make-up a society. When people are guided by the norms of their society to deprive some portion of the population of their civil rights, it will be difficult for anyone in that portion to escape the deprivation, and so a social pattern of injustice will result.

II. The Rule of Law

The connection of civil rights to the rule of law is a

close one. In particular, where the rule of law does not exist in a society due to the fact that some part of the population enjoys special legal privileges, then other parts of the population will be denied their civil rights. But what is the rule of law, and why does its absence mean the denial of civil rights for some?

The rule of law exists in a society when, to a reasonable approximation, persons and groups generally act within the framework of what the laws of the society permit, prohibit, and authorize. The legal framework both constrains and empowers officials and all other members of society. Officials are empowered, for example, to enact and apply laws. Private parties are empowered to form legally-binding contracts and to get married. At the same time, the enactment of laws and other official acts must conform to certain legal procedures in order to be legally valid, and contracts and marriages must conform to certain conditions specified by the laws in order to be legally recognized.

Under the rule of law, the laws have certain features. In particular, they are impersonal, public, positive, and general. Let us look more closely at these features.

The impersonality of laws means that they are not an expression of the will of any particular person or group —neither a prince, nor a nobility, nor any privileged individual or class. Accordingly, in obeying the laws, no one is manifesting a *personal* dependence on anyone else, that is, the kind of dependence that a serf has on his lord or a slave on her owner. Moreover, laws are publicly promulgated so that all can know what they are and regulate their conduct in accordance with their terms. Laws are "positive," in the sense that they are posited by human action, rather than being commandments of a deity or inscribed in the immutable nature of things.

The generality of the laws is not merely a feature of individual laws, with each law applying to some portion of the population defined by general categories, rather than being directed at individuals. More importantly, generality is a characteristic of the totality of laws: the system does not create a society segmented into distinct groups, each with its own distinctive set of legal privileges and immunities, but rather everyone is "equal under the law," as the phrase goes.

A good way to understand the generality of laws is by contrast with the legal arrangements that existed in France and elsewhere in Europe in the centuries before the French Revolution. Those societies rested on legal inequality. Persons had legal rights and immunities, but the bundle of legal claims a person could make was a function of the particular social category to which he belonged. A privileged member of society enjoyed a much more valuable bundle than did any of the remaining members, and, in that sense, society was a system of differential privileges rather than a regime of equal rights.

Thus, guild members and their apprentices had a right to practice a particular craft, while everyone else was prohibited from doing so. Adherents of the dominant religion had full rights of worship, while religious minorities were either not tolerated at all or were subjected to disabilities, such as being excluded from various occupations and required to worship in private spaces. The members of the nobility were immune from taxes imposed upon commoners and had legal powers to exercise jurisdiction over their lands and the persons residing on them. And so on. In this system of privileges, the distinction between being French (or English etc.) and being a foreigner, though not entirely insignificant, did not carry the overriding importance that it would later come to have. Instead, the critical social distinctions were between the nobility and commoners, Protestants and Roman Catholics, and so on.

The French Revolution dramatically transformed society. The National Assembly abolished privileges, with the aim of changing France into a society under the rule of law. Emmanuel Joseph Sieyès, a major intellectual and political figure of the revolution, formulated his vision of the new society at the outset of the transformation: "I picture the law as being in the center of a huge globe; all citizens, without exception, stand equidistant from it on the surface; all are equally dependent on the law; all present to it their liberty and their property; and this is what I call the common rights of citizens" (1789/2014: 111).

Additionally, the French Revolution introduced the principle of "careers open to talents," as it is called. The Declaration of the Rights of Man and of the Citizen (1789) formulated the principle this way: "All citizens, being equal in the eyes of the law, are equally eligible to all dignities and to all public positions and occupations, according to their abilities, and without distinction except that of their virtues and talents" (para. 6). Individual merit, rather than inherited privilege or pre-assigned social status, was to be the basis for social rewards.

The revolution's transformation of France into a society under the rule of law was incomplete in crucial ways. Prominent among the deficiencies was the relegation of women to the status of so-called "passive citizens." Sieyès drew a distinction between active and passive citizenship, and the distinction was taken up by the legal system of the revolutionary regime. He wrote, "Women, at least at present, children, foreigners, those who contribute nothing to support the public establishment must not have an active influence on the direction of the state … [O]nly those who contribute to the public establishment are the real stockholders in the great business of society. They alone are genuinely active citizens, the authentic members of the association" (1789/2014: 127). Here was the beginning of the strict distinction between civil and political rights (see the next section).

Some women objected to the revolution's relegation of them to the status of second-class citizens. Olympe de Gouges published her Declaration of the Rights of Woman and the Female Citizen (1791) in protest of the new regime's failure to treat women as equal citizens. But her claim for women's equality proved unavailing at the time and would take a century and more to gain traction (see Chapter Six). The crucial point for now is this: the revolution did not, in fact, abolish all forms of legal privilege and so failed to establish the rule of law, because male privilege was maintained and women were thereby denied their rightful claim to equal citizenship.

III. Citizenship as Membership

Citizenship is a kind of membership in a modern society. The rights and obligations that attach to membership vary widely from society to society, but, in a broad sense, membership means that an individual has substantial legal rights to freedom, property, and security and can effectively call on the authorities to protect his rights.

There can be different levels of citizenship: As we have just seen, in France, the revolution that brought equal citizenship to (many) men, including —for a time— Jews, made women second-class, "passive" citizens. Men who met certain property qualifications were given the most extensive set of legal rights offered by the country, including rights of political participation. Indigent men and all women were denied political rights.

Slaves were not regarded as members at all by the societies in which they lived, even when their labor was essential to the economy and they comprised a majority of the population. In San Domingue (later Haiti) on the eve of the revolution that began in 1791, the vast majority were slaves. Even though there was legislation prohibiting the abuse of slaves, the law was not enforced and, importantly, slaves had no legal standing to submit a complaint against their abuse. Slave owners literally could and did get away with murder, not to mention torture and a host of inhumane practices aimed at terrorizing their human property into total submission.

Historically, citizenship has also involved special obligations, in particular, the obligation to serve in the armed forces of one's country. One common argument made against extending the full rights of citizenship to women was that, on account of their physical and psychological nature, they were unsuitable for military service. And a common argument against citizenship for European Jews was that they were not suited for such service due to their alleged lack of loyalty to the states in which they resided and to the infeasibility of the military accommodating Jewish dietary rules.

The rights of citizenship, once granted, can be taken away. History is not a one-way ratchet when it comes to civil rights. The revolutionary French government issued a decree in 1794 abolishing slavery in the country's colonies. Eight years later, Napoleon rescinded the decree and restored slavery to Martinique and Guadeloupe, while the expeditionary force that he sent across the Atlantic with the aim of restoring slavery to San Domingue was defeated only by the armed efforts of local Blacks and persons of color. Jews were emancipated by the French Revolution from their servile status and made equal citizens, only to have Napoleon's "Infamous Decree" (1808) take away certain of their civil rights, imposing residency restrictions and subjecting Jewish businesses to special regulations and government supervision.

So civil rights, in the sense of legally recognized entitlements, can be granted by the ruling powers and then rescinded by them. Additionally, when rights are granted, they can be in a form that is limited and qualified in ways that stop well short of what persons are entitled to receive. With the French Revolution, the idea of civil rights first became a major political force in history, but the idea, as it was implemented in law and policy at the time, fell well short of reaching its logical conclusion.

IV. Political Self-Determination

The human population of the modern world has come to be divided almost entirely into politically-independent, territorially-demarcated states, each with the sovereign power under international law to determine its own affairs, subject to the obligations they have voluntarily undertaken, the requirements of the laws of war, and a few demands like the prohibition on genocide that are categorically binding on all states. But along the way to this international system, some sovereign states engaged in ambitious and murderous imperialist ventures in which they subjugated, oppressed, and exploited foreign populations. European states were especially prominent in the story of imperialism, but China, Japan and the U.S. were not entirely innocent in this matter. Additionally, the Ottoman and Russian Empires ruled over many nationalities that had been forcibly incorporated into their realms.

With the Allied victory in World War I, American President Woodrow Wilson promised political self-determination for the subjugated and oppressed peoples of the world. He said that his program for peace reflected "the principle of justice to all peoples and nationalities, and their right to live on equal terms of liberty and safety with one another" (1918). But it turned out that, in practice, he meant only European peoples, and, even then, the realization of his principle of justice was substantially hedged and limited by political compromises.

After World War II, the British withdrew from India as a result of Gandhi's campaign of nonviolent resistance. But the British held on to their other colonies, as did the French and the Dutch. And so within a span of little more than a decade and overlapping with crucial years of the Civil Rights Movement in the U.S., many subjugated populations across Asia and Africa pursued armed campaigns to gain independence from their imperialist overlords and to win political self-determination for themselves. The anti-colonialist movements of the 20th century took Wilson's principle of political self-determination more seriously than he ever did. Those movements raise the question: Is the right of political self-determination a civil right?

Political self-determination in its fullest version is a matter of a population forming a sovereign state and so deciding for itself how it is to be governed, rejecting the rule of any power that might seek to impose its dominion. In a less complete form, self-determination can involve local or regional autonomy for some segment of the population within a centralized sovereign state. But it is often the case that efforts to achieve regional autonomy are intertwined in complex ways with questions about full self-determination. The failure of a central state to grant robust regional autonomy can fuel movements for full self-determination, while, conversely, the granting of robust autonomy can take the steam out of those movements. At the same time, when a substantial portion of a region's population believes that the region is mistreated by the central government, there is always some part of the population that will settle for nothing less than full independence, arguing that it is the only way to stop the mistreatment. The history of Catalonia and its arrangements with the central government of Spain over the past century illustrate these political complexities when it comes to issues of regional autonomy.

Whatever form political self-determination takes, the right to it is necessarily a collective right, held by a population and not by an individual. It was the Vietnamese people as a whole that had the right to throw off the yoke of the French and establish their own regime. And the French did not simply act wrongly in seeking to maintain their control of Vietnam; they wronged the Vietnamese people by not allowing them to collectively decide how to run their own political affairs. Similarly, if the people of Scotland have a right to secede from the United Kingdom and form their own sovereign state, then the right is a collective one held by the people and the denial of the right would do wrong to the people as a whole.

Admittedly, the question of how a people can make

decisions involving its right of self-determination is a complex one. When the political independence of a population is the issue, a plebiscite would be the central part of the process, assuming that a free and fair vote is possible as a practical matter. But often such a vote is not possible. And, even when it is possible, there are difficult questions concerning whether or not a decision to secede requires a supermajority or, as suggested by some thinkers, two plebiscites separated by several years and a turnout that exceeds 50% of the eligible voters. Catalonia's troubled relation to the central authorities in Madrid illustrate not only the political difficulties surrounding the question of how a people makes decisions regarding its collective self-determination, but also the conceptual and ethical complexities in determining what the people have actually decided.

In contrast to the collective nature of the right of political self-determination, civil rights are standardly understood as individual rights that are essentially concerned with the freedom of the individual to make decisions for himself and to live a life in which his basic interests are protected by his state. And so a conceptual distinction can be drawn between civil rights and the right of political self-determination. However, this distinction, even if valid, does not mean that the two kinds of rights are unrelated. The rights to vote and hold public office are civil rights held by individuals, even though they bear on the collective political self-determination of a nation and shape the form that its self-determination can legitimately take. Yet, it is worth pursuing the question of whether or not the right of self-determination, even though collective in nature, should also be counted as a civil right. Just as history has shown that such traditional civil rights as those involving freedom to travel and hold property were insecure for individuals who lacked political rights, it also shows that when societies are ruled by an alien nation, the ruling powers routinely trample on the individual rights of the members of the subjugated society. In practice, the elimination of colonial rule and other forms of alien political domination is almost always a necessary condition, even if not a sufficient one, for securing individual civil rights. So by parity of reasoning with the case for counting the right to vote as a civil right, one can argue that the right of political self-determination should also count as a civil right.

Nonetheless, it makes sense to distinguish the question 'What are the rights to which each individual citizen of a modern state is entitled *qua* citizen?' from the question 'Which populations have a right of political self-determination?' Part of the answer to the latter question will be: those populations that are willing and able to construct and maintain a state that adequately protects the rights to which each individual citizen of a modern state is entitled. Civil rights can thus be understood as providing criteria for determining which populations validly claim a right to political self-determination. So understood, civil rights are reasonably distinguished from the right for which they provide criteria. For that reason, it is probably best to say that the right of political self-determination is not a civil right, notwithstanding the normative and practical connections between the two sorts of rights.

Chapter 3

Rights: Natural, Human, and Civil

I. Natural Rights

The idea of rights plays a central role in the moral and political discourse of the 21st century. Such has not always been the case. In ancient times, the foci of moral and normative political discussion were justice, goodness, and excellence. Then, as Christianity spread through Europe, the ideas of sin, evil, and redemption became central. But by the end of the 18th century, the idea of rights had become a major part of the conversation. Talk of natural rights, inalienable rights, the rights of man, and human rights served to shape thinking about how persons should treat one another and how society should be organized. The American Declaration of Independence (1776) invoked the "unalienable rights" with which God had endowed all men: life, liberty and the pursuit of happiness. The French Declaration of the Rights of Man and of the Citizen (1789) spoke of "the natural and imprescriptible rights of man," namely, "liberty, property, security, and resistance to oppression." And although the French Declaration did not clearly distinguish natural from civil rights (i.e., the rights of man from those of the citizen), it was more responsible than any other political document for making the idea of civil rights a key one in the political history of modernity.

In order to understand the connection between natural and civil rights, let us examine in more detail the idea of natural rights and why some thinkers over the centuries have seen the idea as problematic, despite its influence. To begin, it is helpful to disentangle two features that are traditionally ascribed to natural rights: 1) their validity does not depend on the existence of any laws, norms, or directives that are made by humans, and 2) they are part of the fabric of nature.

The first feature holds that the prohibitions and freedoms that go along with natural rights are the grounds of valid demands, regardless of any norms or directives whose source is what some humans have done or said. That individuals have a natural right against being enslaved means that they can make a valid demand against their enslavers, even if the laws and customs of a society (or most societies or even every society) license slavery. The second feature of natural rights is that they are inherent in nature, where 'nature' is broadly understood to include human nature. The idea is that human nature is the same in everyone and that this universally shared nature precedes any particular processes of socialization and acculturation and persists even as those processes overlay the substrate that is common to all humans.

This view of human nature is expressed by Christian Wilhelm von Dohm, a Prussian civil servant who published a revolutionary tract in 1781 in which he argued that Jews should be granted all the civil rights enjoyed by Christians, making them equal citizens of the states they inhabited. Dohm recognized that the traditional beliefs, practices, and personal appearance of Europe's Jews made them different from the Christian majority in very noticeable ways. And, indeed, Jews were widely regarded by European Christians as an alien people who did not fit in with mainstream European society and culture and were not loyal to the states in which they resided. So why did it make sense to give such a people the rights of citizens? In a key part of his argument, Dohm wrote that "[t]he Jew is even more man than Jew" (28) and "human nature is the same in all people" (34). He thought that Jews had the same natural rights as all other humans because they were in essence the same as all other humans and that their human nature would turn them into loyal and valuable citizens if only they were given the rights of citizenship (see Chapter Five for further discussion of Dohm's argument).

Not everyone was happy with the rights-talk that was sweeping Western Europe and America at the end of the 18th century. Unsurprisingly, defenders of the status quo regarded such talk as a threat, because rights were often claimed by those who were subordinated, seeking radical changes in society. But even some critics of the status quo, such as the utilitarian philosopher Jeremy Bentham, rejected the rights talk that accompanied the French Revolution in particular.

Bentham had no problems with the idea of legal rights. Those were rights that had a tangible existence in the way the machinery of government —legislatures, courts, police etc.— operated. And legal rights provided safety and security for the members of society. But for Bentham's empirical cast of mind, the matter was much different when it came to rights that were alleged to have validity prior to, and independent of, any government or set of rules laid down by society. Rights of precisely that kind were at the center of America's Declaration of Independence and France's Declaration of Rights. Those were rights thought to be built into the nature of things, akin in that way to Newton's laws of motion and gravity, and claimed to be imprescriptible —not susceptible to being abrogated or restricted by any power.

Bentham denied the existence of natural rights and asserted that the very idea of such rights was "nonsense" (1843: 6369). Moreover, the idea was dangerous to society, because it licensed every person and group to disobey the law, and even to foment revolution, on the ground that the law and government were guilty of violating their natural rights. In Bentham's view, it was only law and government that made a safe and secure life possible for anyone, and so talk of natural rights constituted, for him, a clear and present danger to any social order. Even the social order that the French revolutionaries sought to establish was undermined by the very talk of rights that inspired their revolution.

For Bentham, clear-headed moral thinking rested on his principle of utility, which demanded that every action and law promote the greatest good for the greatest number. Any rights that failed to meet this demand must be limited or eliminated. Bentham did not find this kind of thinking in the French Declaration, and he contended that the advocates of a natural right to liberty failed to grasp that all rights restrict liberty.

However, Bentham's assumption that the natural right to liberty amounts to an unbounded right to do anything one pleases is not part of the natural rights tradition. Rather, the tradition draws a distinction between liberty and license. To be sure, sound moral reasoning is needed to determine what the boundaries of the right to liberty are, and, as we will see shortly, deficient reasoning can lead natural-rights thinking far astray. But, *contra* Bentham, one can hold that there is a natural right to liberty without committing oneself to the implausible view that the right is unbounded.

Moreover, Bentham appears oblivious to the fact that the right to liberty was first and foremost a right against being enslaved or reduced to degraded and servile status. Moreover, there is a world of difference between invoking Bentham's principle of utility and asserting, "We enslaved persons demand our freedom because abolishing slavery will serve the greatest good for the greatest number," and, instead, declaring, "We demand our freedom because our enslavement violates the right to liberty that we possess as human beings." The former statement strikes a false note, to say the least, because it fails to register the special position that the enslaved are in with respect to slavery. Slavery is not simply very bad from some detached perspective that surveys the good of each; slavery does grievous wrong to the enslaved, and the invocation of rights gives voice to this special moral position of the enslaved.

It is true that natural rights are not part of the empirical world in the way that legal rights are. Natural rights are moral norms, not facts; they represent what morally ought to be, not what is. But as empirically-minded as he was, Bentham did not escape the world of moral norms. His own principle of utility was such a norm and not an entirely unproblematic one, as the example of slavery shows.

To be sure, the idea of natural rights is also problematic. Such rights are not, *pace* Bentham, unbounded, but their scope and boundaries are not self-defining and require sound moral reasoning to determine. Absent such reasoning, the idea of natural rights might lead one morally far astray. For example, John Locke, a central figure in the development of the natural rights tradition, believed that the natural right to freedom was compatible with slavery and, in particular, with the slave system being established during his lifetime in North America. He argued that persons engaging in an unjust war had forfeited their right to life and, when taken captive by those they fought, legitimately became slaves of their captors (1690/1952: para. 85). But Locke offered no explanation of how those who took Africans captive were engaged in a just war against them, nor an account of why the children of the original captives could be legitimately enslaved. Subsequent natural-rights thinkers understood the defects in Locke's reasoning that led him to ignore the contradiction between slavery and natural rights, and arguments based on natural rights became a key part of anti-slavery views.

The two free persons of color from San Domingue who appeared before the French National Convention in 1794 to ask that body to affirm the abolition of slavery invoked the rights of man that the French Declaration had proclaimed. Toussaint Louverture, the ex-slave who would become ruler of San Domingue, repeatedly invoked those same rights. In America, as early as the 1770's, slaves petitioned state governments, asking for emancipation on the basis of their natural right to freedom. David Walker's fiery abolitionist pamphlet declared that "we [American Blacks] ask ... for nothing but the rights of man" (1830: 75). And, in denouncing the enslavement of Africans and their offspring, Frederick Douglass wrote, "Human rights stand upon a common basis; and by all the reason that they are supported, maintained, and defended, for one variety of the human family, they are supported, maintained, and defended for *all* the human family" (1854/2016: 245; emphasis in original). Douglass was writing as part of a natural rights tradition that included the deficient version found in Locke but also the more adequate understanding that found voice in many abolitionist writings.

II. The Socialist Critique of Rights

Civil rights are individual rights, but more than a few thinkers have had serious reservations about individual rights, whether understood as moral or legal claims. An influential critique of rights is found in the socialist tradition, which regarded the very idea of individual rights as tied inextricably to capitalism and as antagonistic to the kind of society that would emerge under socialist arrangements. The classic text on this matter is Marx's "On the Jewish Question" (1843).

Marx's essay was a response to a book by the philosopher Bruno Bauer. Bauer's *The Jewish Problem (Question)* addressed the issue of what Christian society should do with the Jews in its midst. The process of Jewish emancipation was underway in much of Europe at the time, as Jews and their allies pressed for states to eliminate the legal restrictions imposed on their Jewish populations and to establish equal citizenship for Jews.

Bauer rejected the idea of a specifically Jewish emancipation. He asserted that Jews were selfish in demanding emancipation for themselves, when even Christians lacked the full set of civil and political rights to which persons were entitled. Moreover, Bauer claimed that Jews stubbornly adhered to "antiquated traditions" and had "placed themselves against the wheel of history" (1843/1958: 4 and 5), with the result that science and progress had no place within their mentality. Bauer was no Christian, and he regarded Christianity as a piece of mythology and thought that true freedom for all would require everyone to give up their religion. But in Bauer's eyes, Christianity at least had a universal message of human equality, while Judaism rested on the separatist idea that the Jews alone were God's chosen people.

Marx's essay drew a distinction between political emancipation and full human emancipation. The distinction rested on the fact that "a state may be a free state without man himself being a free man" (1843/1978: 32). A free state was one in which all citizens enjoyed a full set of individual rights, including rights to religious liberty, private property and the franchise. Marx wrote, "Political emancipation certainly represents great progress ... [and] is the final form of human emancipation within the framework of the prevailing social order" (35). Yet, political emancipation "is not the final and absolute form of human emancipation" (32), because the prevailing order was based on egoism and the pursuit of private material gain.

For Marx, the final form of human emancipation would be achieved only when egoism and the pursuit of private gain were transcended, and all persons were committed to the good of each one. In such a society, individual rights would be unnecessary and even harmful: unnecessary because the function of rights, as Marx saw it, was to enable individuals to protect themselves against other, egoistically-motivated individuals; harmful, because rights, as individual possessions, put persons in an antagonistic relation to one another.

Marx thought that Bauer's criticisms of Jews were wrongly focused on their religious ideas, specifically their idea of themselves as God's chosen people. For Marx, what mattered was what Jews actually did, and here Marx, no less than Bauer, gave voice to the anti-Semitic attitudes of his day: "Money is the jealous god of Israel" (50). Jews worshipped Mammon, Marx was saying. And he added a twist, contending that Jewish money-worship "has become the practical spirit of the Christian nations ... [and] the Christians have become Jews" (49). A version of the twist would become a familiar anti-Semitic trope, still heard to this day: Jews had covertly taken control of Christian society. In any event, for Marx, full emancipation for both Jews and Christians would occur only when society transcended egoism.

Much of the socialist tradition following from Marx embraced his view of rights as protections needed only in a society dominated by egoism. To be sure, socialists advocated, at various points, civil and political rights for working men and women. But such rights were seen as transitory measures that would be left behind once socialism was firmly established and the state had withered away.

The Italian thinker Carlo Rosselli was virtually a lone voice when he argued in the 1930's for a liberal socialism that would incorporate protections for individual rights, not as a transitory prelude to a socialist society where persons would need no such protections but as an essential element of socialism, demanded by the respect that is owed to each human (1930/1994). In more recent decades, liberal socialism —commonly called "democratic socialism"— has emerged as an important part of socialist thought. The German philosopher Axel Honneth is one of many contemporary socialists who have proposed a revised form of socialism that departs from traditional versions when it comes to individual rights (2015). Honneth explains that early socialists failed to appreciate the emancipatory and enduring role of civil rights. Such rights are essential to the democratic processes through which persons with divergent views of law and policy collectively decide how their polity is to be governed. Socialism cannot legitimately displace or supersede those processes but must incorporate them. Thus, on Honneth's account, the protection of civil rights remains an indispensable feature of any legitimate form of socialism.

III. The Universal Declaration of Human Rights

The Universal Declaration of Human Rights (1948) was a document unanimously affirmed by the member states of the United Nations in the wake of the unprecedented death and destruction of World War II. In its preamble, the declaration proclaimed that "recognition of the inherent dignity and of the equal and inalienable rights of all members of the human family is the foundation of freedom, justice and peace in the world" and that "human rights should be protected by the rule of law."

The declaration proceeded to enumerate a large number of rights. The most general of them were the rights to life, liberty and security of the person. Many of the remainder can be understood as concerned with various aspects of those general rights. The list includes the rights against slavery, servitude, torture, and cruel, inhuman, or degrading treatment; the rights to equality before the law and protection against discrimination; the rights against arbitrary arrest, detention, and exile; the right to a fair judicial process if accused of a crime; the right to freedom of movement and to get married and begin a family; the rights to property, freedom of conscience, expression, and religion and to freedom of association. Also included are the rights to work and to have access to an education.

Additionally, the declaration proclaimed, "Everyone has the right to a nationality" (Article 15). This provision appears to mean that every human has the right to be the citizen of some state, though no specification is given of what determines which particular state an individual is entitled to hold citizenship in. The unstated assumption is that there are particular facts about an individual —where she was born, what the citizenship was of her parents, or some other fact establishing a connection to the state in question— that determine where she is entitled to citizenship.

The declaration was, in an important way, a civil rights document as much as it was a charter of human rights. Implicitly addressing all states, it asserted, "Everyone is entitled to all the rights and freedoms set forth in this Declaration, without distinction of any kind, such as race, color, sex, language, religion, political or other opinion, national or social origin, property, birth or other status" (Article 2). The enumerated rights made explicit which protections citizens were owed by their state. Humans had the rights simply in virtue of being human, but they were also entitled to the protections of a specific state in virtue of particular facts about them that linked them to the state.

The declaration was met with skepticism in some quarters. During the drafting process, the American Anthropological Association (AAA) published a statement in which it expressed its reservations. The association was concerned that the declaration would simply be a statement of the principles of Western societies parading as universally valid values. Underlying this concern was the history of European and American imperialism, which the association condemned for the grievous harm it did to the peoples who had been subjected to imperialist hegemony. Western powers rationalized their conduct by invoking the doctrine of "the White-man's burden," the idea that Whites had a responsibility to civilize peoples of color. But this deeply racist idea had been "disastrous for mankind" (AAA 1947: 540). Even after the conclusion of World War II, Britain, France and other European nations sought to hold on to their colonies. The association's worry about imperialism was by no means an idle one.

At the same time, the association apparently endorsed a form of ethical relativism, asserting that "[s]tandards and values are relative to the culture from which they derive" (542). As for states that oppress a foreign population, the association wrote that "underlying cultural values may be called on to bring the peoples of such states to a realization of the consequences of the acts of their governments, and thus enforce a brake upon discrimination and conquest. For the political system of a people is only a small part of their total culture" (543).

However, it was not simply the political systems of Western imperialist countries that supported the discrimination and conquest that the association rightly found morally repellent. The racist cultural values of those countries —including the idea of the White-man's burden— lent their unwavering support. Additionally, it is unclear how the AAA could reconcile its relativism with its condemnation of imperialism.

A half a century after expressing its skepticism about the Universal Declaration, the AAA voiced a different view (1999). The association explicitly abandoned its previous relativism, asserting that it had a responsibility to oppose every culture that denies its members the realization of their humanity. The association went on to say that this responsibility "implies starting from the baseline of the Universal Declaration ... and associated implementing international legislation, but also expanding the definition of human rights to include areas not necessarily addressed by international law" (1999). One should take note that expanding the definition of human rights invariably enlarges the grounds on which cultures can be criticized for violating such rights. The association has thereby travelled a long way from its earlier reluctance to endorse an international human rights document.

In any event, the AAA failed to distinguish two ways of understanding the Universal Declaration: 1) as a document that embodies a particular metaphysical view of the human person and of the moral values that go along with that view, and 2) as a document that is not committed to any particular metaphysical view of the person but is committed to the idea that certain ways of treating persons are morally intolerable and that there are very strong moral and practical reasons for holding states accountable if they perpetrate or permit such treatment. Let me elaborate on each understanding.

According to the first understanding, the declaration reflects a view according to which the essential feature of human personhood is the capacity of the individual to separate himself in thought and action from any social ties that he might have and any ideas that he might accept at a given time. This capacity manifests itself in the individual's questioning whether or not the social ties are good ones for him to have and the ideas sufficiently persuasive for him to accept. The capacity is also manifested when the individual, on reflection, reaffirms his social ties, or breaks them, and endorses his ideas, or rejects them. The moral perspective that goes along with this view is one that takes the highest moral requirement to be the demand to protect the individual in the exercise of this essential capacity of human personhood. In other words, the supreme demand is the protection of individual autonomy. The rights enumerated in the declaration are then understood as rights tied to the person's exercise of autonomy: the rights provide each individual with the moral space and the opportunities to manifest what is essential to his human personhood. Accordingly, the declaration reflects an individualist perspective, on this first interpretation.

Construed in this first way, the declaration would be rightly subject to the criticism that it reflects a way of thinking that is foreign to much of the world and so is unlikely to achieve the practical aim of the drafters to have the declaration endorsed by societies around the globe. The way of thinking in question has had its deepest impact on Western societies, although it should be noted that, even there, large segments of the population accept it only equivocally, at best. In other societies, the individualist metaphysical and moral perspective has much less purchase on people's thought and action and on the organization of society. Separation and questioning counts less in understanding what is essential to human personhood and what is good for human beings than connection, community, and tradition.

On the second interpretation of the declaration, the document embodies moral ideas and values, to be sure, but ones that are more broadly shared across modern societies than are the individualist values of the first understanding. A committee of philosophers that the U.N. formed in 1947 had been given the task of addressing the very matter of whether or not a declaration of rights could be agreed upon across a suitably broad range of societies and concluded that certain rights "may be seen as implicit in man's nature as an individual and as a member of society and to follow from the fundamental right to live" (Glendon: 77). The second understanding of the declaration regards it as spelling out, to some approximation, those broadly acceptable rights.

The key thought behind this second understanding is that, in contrast to traditional theories of natural rights, no particular metaphysical view of human personhood, community, or the cosmos is needed to affirm (most of) the rights enumerated in the declaration. Rather, a range of otherwise conflicting views can converge in affirming the document, because each view can see the enumerated rights as serving a very valuable function. In particular, individualist as well as communitarian perspectives can agree that, in order for humans in modern societies to lead lives that are reasonably fulfilling and free of undue suffering and hardship, it is generally necessary for the rights spelled out in the declaration to be respected and protected.

This second understanding of the declaration makes the moral viewpoint of the document more capacious than the first interpretation, capable of embracing a broader range of the particular metaphysical and moral perspectives that can be found across cultures. Such catholicity serves the practical aim of having the declaration endorsed by societies around the world. But the catholicity can also be seen as a moral virtue, demonstrating due respect for the diversity of societies and helping to prevent the kinds of moral calamities that have been a recurrent feature of human history.

IV. The Right to Have Rights

Writing in the wake of the Second World War, the philosopher Hannah Arendt distinguished the rights of man from civil rights, criticizing the former while affirming the latter. The rights of man were natural rights and, during the first half of the 20th century, had proven to be of no practical value to those persons who invoked them for protection. Reflecting upon the interwar and postwar periods, Arendt wrote, "The Rights of Man, supposedly inalienable, proved to be unenforceable ... whenever people appeared who were no longer citizens of any sovereign state" (1948/1994: 293). She argued that the persons who lacked effective citizenship in any state —those rendered stateless by the political upheavals of both world wars, as well as the survivors of the Nazi death camps— found that natural rights had failed them and "could see ... that the abstract nakedness of being nothing but human was their greatest danger" (300). Arendt, a Jewish refugee from Nazi Germany who became a naturalized U.S. citizen after the war, was herself one of the many whom natural rights had failed. It is unsurprising, then, that she postulated "[t]he end of the rights of man" (267).

By contrast with natural rights, civil rights were secured by the law and government of a particular state, and, importantly, they were secured only for the citizens of the state in question. For Arendt, a critical feature of civil rights was that there was a machinery of enforcement behind them, a machinery of laws and government that was lacking in the case of natural rights. To address the perilous situation of stateless persons, she introduced the idea of "a right to have rights" (296-97). The idea referred to a right to belong to a political community that would secure individual rights for its members. Because those individual rights were backed by a machinery of enforcement, they were not ineffective abstractions like natural rights but rather concrete and effective claims.

Unlike Bentham, Arendt was not claiming that the very idea of natural rights was nonsensical. Her contention was that the idea was a colossal practical failure, leaving unprotected millions of people. Against Arendt, it might be said that the idea of civil rights, too, had been an utter failure in the case of America's free Blacks prior to the Civil War and all of the nation's Blacks from the end of Reconstruction to the signal victories of the Civil Rights Movement (see Chapter Four). The machinery of enforcement was decidedly ineffective in protecting the rights of Blacks. Still, one can acknowledge such failures and also agree with Arendt that, for almost all humans in the modern world —including America's Blacks— citizenship in a functioning state is a necessary condition as a practical matter for having any of one's rights made secure.

However, Arendt left unclarified the status of her "right to have rights." The right is not a civil right: it is the right *to be* a citizen and not one of the rights *of being* a citizen. But neither is the right to have rights a natural right, in Arendt's view: she did not subject the right to the criticisms she makes of natural rights, nor did she regard it as falling under her declaration of the end of the rights of man. She thought that the right was not over and done with, but rather that it was of continuing and crucial importance.

However, it is difficult to see Arendt's right to have rights as anything but a right that, like any natural right, belongs to humans in their "abstract nakedness" (299), because it is a right held by all persons, including those who are not members of any political community. Her right thus appears to be, not an alternative to natural rights, but a newly declared natural right. Moreover, the idea of a right to have rights has little conceptual content or practical meaning in the absence of some specification of the rights to which one is entitled. Leaving the specification of content entirely at the discretion of each state would be highly questionable, especially in light of the long history of racial, ethnic, and religious discrimination practiced by many states. So it seems that the Universal Declaration and other human rights documents can do important work in giving content to Arendt's idea of a right to have rights. At the same time, it must be acknowledged that, at the international level, the machinery for enforcing human rights is sorely lacking and that humans remain almost entirely dependent on the law and government of the states to which they belong to secure their human rights.

Chief Justice of the U.S. Supreme Court Earl Warren struck an Arendtian note when he wrote, "Citizenship *is* man's basic right, for it is nothing less than the right to have rights. Remove this priceless possession and there remains a stateless person, disgraced and degraded in the eyes of his countrymen" (Perez v. Brownell 1958: 64; emphasis in original). But Warren's claim that citizenship is the basic right of a human being is conceptually and morally problematic. The rights to which a human being has the right are conceptually more basic, because the latter right depends on them but not vice versa. And morally speaking, it would seem that the right not to be enslaved, for example, is at least as basic as the right to be a citizen of a state that protects one against slavery. At the same time, in an era when the international order consists of politically-independent, modern states, a right to citizenship has crucial practical importance, and those persons who lack citizenship in any functioning state are generally in a situation of extreme precariousness and have a legitimate claim based on their being human to become citizens of a state.

Chapter 4

The Fight of American Blacks for Freedom and Equality

I. Slavery

In many instances of the systemic denial of civil rights, the victims still have some socially-recognized and legally-supported rights. But that was not the case with slaves under the systems of chattel slavery found in such places as the antebellum U.S. and the Caribbean colonies of France and Britain. Under those systems, the slave could not call on the authorities for protection: she was subject to the arbitrary will of her owner. Invoking "[t]he established habits and uniform practice of the country," the North Carolina Supreme Court wrote in 1829, "We cannot allow the right of the master [over the slave] to be brought into discussion in the courts of justice. The slave, to remain a slave, must be made sensible that there is no appeal from his master" (State v. Mann: 265 and 267). Indeed, the authorities licensed the arbitrary power of the slaveholder over his human property and were at the call of the owner should his property escape or otherwise seek to assert her own will. The slave's life was thus suffused by a profound subjection to the will of another.

Moreover, slaves were regarded as having no interests of their own that counted for anything in the eyes of the broader society. So their will counted for nothing, and their interests counted for nothing. Insofar as full personhood involves being socially recognized as having a will of one's own that is entitled to respect and having interests that matter, we can say that chattel slavery involved the radical rejection of the slave's personhood. This rejection meant that, although the slave interacted with members of the society, he was in no way regarded as himself a member. Rather, the slave was "socially dead" (Patterson 1982: 5-10 and 38) and existed at the opposite end of the spectrum from persons who enjoyed the full set of civil rights. Emblematic of the slave's social death was the denial of his right to get married, raise children, or inherit property: society is a multigenerational enterprise, and the slave was treated as though he was not part of that enterprise in that the broader society did not recognize any of the slave's ties to ancestors and children.

The language of emancipation has been prevalent in many civil rights movements, because the persons seeking their rights have perceived their situation as analogous in morally significant respects to that of slaves. The conditions of those persons have not amounted to slavery, but it is sensible to think of their situation, at least in some cases, as similar to slavery insofar as the protestors are objecting to conditions and treatment that amount to a severe denial of their agency and interests and reduce them to a servile status. To be an equal citizen of a modern state is, in the first place, not to be a slave, and the denial of equal citizenship has often meant being treated by prevailing social and legal norms in a way that is akin in certain respects to the treatment that constituted the degraded and servile status of the slave.

II. The Antebellum Civil Rights Movement

In his infamous opinion for the U.S. Supreme Court in Dred Scott v. Sandford (1857), Chief Justice Roger B. Taney declared that, according to the customs and laws of the country, all persons of African ancestry —whether slave or free— were "so far inferior [to whites] that they had no rights which the white man was bound to respect" (Finkelman: 2017: 61). In Taney's view, the country was formed by a social contract exclusively among Whites, for the exclusive benefit of Whites. Northern states had extended some legal rights to free Blacks, but Taney thought that such rights were granted purely at the discretion of Whites, and nothing in the country's laws or customs prohibited the withdrawal of those rights by the states, for whatever reason Whites deemed sufficient.

Taney's view of American laws and customs was distorted by his own proslavery attitude: he seized upon certain prominent strands in the nation's history and laws, while ignoring significant countervailing norms in some parts of the country, such as the repeal by Massachusetts of its anti-miscegenation law in 1843. Yet, it still must be recognized that, although free Blacks in the antebellum period were not slaves, throughout the country they lived under restrictions and burdens that were not placed on Whites.

Southern states were particularly draconian in limiting the liberties of free Blacks. When travelling through the region, free Blacks were legally required to carry official papers proving that they were free, on pain of being sent into slavery. South Carolina had a law providing for the detention of all free Black seamen who were temporarily in the state. Virginia adopted legislation that required all manumitted slaves to leave the state. While a number of southern states prohibited the teaching of reading and writing to slaves, Georgia's prohibition extended to any Black person, free or enslaved. Georgia also prohibited all Blacks from holding religious meetings of more than seven persons and required a license from local authorities of Blacks wishing to hold a meeting of seven or fewer.

Northern states also severely limited the liberties and rights of free Blacks. Ohio required all Blacks to post bond before entering the state and deprived them of the right to testify in court against Whites. Even as New York emancipated its slaves over several decades at the beginning of the 19th century, it imposed on Blacks a discriminatory property qualification for the franchise. Pennsylvania harbored considerable anti-slavery sentiment, but its 1838 constitution did not extend the right to vote to Blacks.

In the decades preceding the Civil War, free Blacks in the North organized to protest, not only slavery, but also laws and practices throughout the region that denied Blacks their civil and political rights. These protests amounted to the first civil rights movement in the U.S. It involved petitions to state governments, lawsuits, public talks, and articles in anti-slavery newspapers and journals. Free Blacks in Massachusetts and their White abolitionist allies not only denounced slavery and sought to prevent Blacks alleged to be fugitive slaves from being sent into captivity in the South, they worked for the aforementioned repeal of the state's anti-miscegenation law and the elimination of racial segregation in its public schools and transportation. As a result of those efforts, not only was interracial marriage decriminalized, most of the state's passenger railways were desegregated. School desegregation was also achieved in several cities. However, Boston remained a holdout, and, the Supreme Judicial Court of Massachusetts upheld the city's mandated racial separation of its schoolchildren (Roberts v. Boston 1849).

The most urgent civil rights issue for free Blacks in the North during the antebellum period involved the capture and rendition of persons alleged to be fugitive slaves. The federal Fugitive Slave Act of 1793 provided a legal process for slaveholders and their agents to travel into northern states for the purpose of seizing escaped slaves and returning them to captivity. The slavecatchers were to go to local authorities in the North and receive a certificate of removal, authorizing the forcible rendition of the alleged slave.

Congress had enacted the 1793 law under the infamous "Fugitive Slave Clause" of the Constitution, which prohibited any state from emancipating slaves who had escaped from captivity in another state. The clause also obligated all states to return escaped slaves upon the claim of the owner (Article IV, Section 2). The 1793 law left free Blacks in the North in a very precarious position: the law gave them no rights of due process, and courts generally declined to rule that Blacks had such rights under the Due Process Clause of the Constitution. Free Blacks were falsely accused of being escaped slaves, and federal law failed to give them the right to defend themselves or produce evidence of their status as free, much less the right to a jury trial. This blatant violation of civil rights was a direct result of the country's efforts to protect to the fullest feasible extent the legal right of slaveholders to hold their human property in captivity. The civil rights of free Blacks and the moral right to emancipation of slaves were thus inextricably intertwined.

Eventually, some northern states enacted what were called "personal liberty laws," which gave free Blacks rights of due process or otherwise helped to protect them against slavecatchers. For example, Massachusetts (1837) and New York (1840) gave Blacks who were alleged to be fugitive slaves the right to a jury trial. Pennsylvania (1826) made it a crime to use force or violence against any individual with the intention of keeping or selling him as a slave. However, the U.S. Supreme Court struck down the Pennsylvania law and declared as invalid any state law limiting the right of a slaveowner to the immediate possession of his human property (Prigg v. Pennsylvania 1842).

Slaveholders were not satisfied with the court's decision, because it did not obligate state officials to cooperate in the rendition of persons alleged to be escaped slaves. Northern officials, moved by their antislavery sentiments and convictions, sometimes rejected the requests of slavecatchers for certificates of removal. After intense protests and lobbying efforts by slaveholders, Congress enacted the Fugitive Slave Act of 1850.

The law provided for the appointment of federal commissioners authorized to conduct proceedings pursuant to the act and to issue certificates of removal to a purported slaveholder who has produced "satisfactory proof" that a certain Black person was his escaped slave. The certificate would empower the slaveholder "to use such reasonable force and restraint as may be necessary … to take and remove such fugitive person back to the State or Territory whence he or she may have escaped" (sec. 6). The federal commissioners were to be appointed by the President, and, in light of the political alignments of the day, it was clear that the commissioners would be more sympathetic to slaveholders than state officials had been.

Blacks accused of being fugitive slaves were prohibited by the law from testifying in the proceedings, and, in a particularly egregious violation of due process, commissioners would be paid $10 for every case in which they issued a certificate of removal but only $5 for every case in which they declined to issue a certificate. Additionally, the law prohibited courts from issuing a writ of habeas corpus in fugitive slave cases. The "Great Writ," as it was traditionally called in English jurisprudence, was commonly regarded as a crucial legal mechanism for protecting the lawful liberties of individuals. A person who was illegally detained could ask a court to order those detaining him to explain the reasons for the detention. Prior to 1850, Blacks alleged to be escaped slaves and held in detention until they could be forcibly sent to the South could and did ask courts to issue writs of habeas corpus.

The 1850 act also commanded all citizens to assist in the capture and rendition of accused fugitive slaves and provided for criminal penalties against anyone obstructing a slaveholder who sought to arrest his fugitive slave and anyone aiding the escape of a slave detained under the law (sections 5 and 7). The act marked the beginning of a decade that was a particularly grim one for American Blacks. Even as abolitionist sentiment intensified in the North, slaveholders and northerners who were opposed to abolition maintained a tight grip on national politics. And the Supreme Court was decidedly pro-slavery and deeply racist, as made manifest in the Dred Scott case (1857).

Scott had been taken several times by his owner to reside in parts of the country where slavery was legally prohibited, before being returned to the slave state of Missouri. Legal precedent in the state, as well as international law, provided that, once a slave became free, he was always free. But the state Supreme Court overruled the precedent.

When Scott appealed, the U.S. Supreme Court could simply have held that the state's decision was controlling, but it went much further. In his opinion for the court, Chief Justice Taney not only declared that Blacks, free or slave, had no rights that Whites were obligated to respect, but he also proclaimed that no one of African ancestry was, or could ever be, a citizen of the U.S. and that Congress had no legal authority to outlaw slavery in territories held by the national government (much of U.S. territory at the time comprised lands that had not yet become states and were held by the central government).

III. The Aborted Constitutional Revolution

It would take a civil war and three amendments to the Constitution (the "Civil War Amendments") to give American Blacks the legal promise of equal citizenship. The 13th Amendment (1865) abolished slavery; the 14th (1868) made all persons born on American soil citizens of the country and prohibited states from denying any person "the equal protection of the laws," and the 15th (1870) prohibited the denial of the right to vote on account of race.

The revolutionary new legal regime established by the Civil War Amendments might have taken root during "Reconstruction," as the period from 1865 to 1876 is known. During that time, federal troops were stationed in the South to help protect the rights of Blacks, who participated very actively in politics, helping to draft new state constitutions and serving in elected office. More than a dozen Blacks served in Congress. But the large majority of southern Whites were determined, notwithstanding the Civil War Amendments, to establish a system of racial subjugation, degradation, and exploitation that, if not identical to antebellum slavery, was a close cousin. And to that end, many Whites joined the Ku Klux Klan and similar terrorist groups, perpetrating with impunity widespread violence against Blacks. Additionally, the interest of northern Whites in making good on the promises of the Civil War Amendments dissipated.

Reconstruction collapsed in 1877, when federal troops were withdrawn from the South, a result of a back-room political deal that enabled Rutherford B. Hayes to be elected President. The groundwork was thereby set for the development in the South of the White supremacist system of racial subjugation and terror known as "Jim Crow." The system trampled on the constitutional rights of Blacks, severely circumscribing their lawful freedoms and reducing them to a class of menial servants and harshly-exploited agricultural workers barely better off than slaves. At the same time, in the North, Blacks were excluded from trade unions and subjected to discrimination in housing, education, and other areas, although Black subordination was not as comprehensive or violent as it was in the South.

The U.S. Supreme Court was complicit in the collapse of Reconstruction and the consolidation of Jim Crow. In a series of decisions, the court refused to vindicate the civil rights of Blacks, giving implausibly restrictive readings of constitutional protections and the authority of Congress to enforce the protections through legislation. The court not only invalidated important national civil rights laws and licensed states to ignore the rights of Blacks, it also explicitly upheld state laws that helped turn Blacks into a subordinate and stigmatized caste.

In Cruikshank v. U.S (1876), the defendants were convicted under the federal Civil Rights Act of 1870, which made it a crime to conspire "to injure, oppress, threaten, or intimidate any citizen with intent to prevent or hinder his free exercise and enjoyment of any right or privilege granted or secured to him by the constitution" (section 6). The case came from Louisiana and arose out of an armed conflict that ensued when Democrats, whose party opposed racial equality, sought to seize control of a local courthouse in Colfax parish, where Republicans, whose party supported equality, had been elected to govern. Armed Blacks assembled to protect the courthouse, but, finding themselves surrounded and outgunned by a White supremacist paramilitary group, the Blacks surrendered and were taken captive by the group. Many of the Black captives were then murdered in what is now known as the "Colfax massacre." The defendants in Cruikshank participated in those murders, but the state did not prosecute them. However, the federal government brought prosecutions and won convictions.

Yet the U.S. Supreme Court overturned the convictions. The court held that the murders were purely a matter for the state of Louisiana to deal with, as the victims had not had any of their constitutional rights violated. The prosecution argued that the defendants had deprived their victims of the rights to peaceably assemble (First Amendment) and to bear arms (Second Amendment), as well as their right to equal protection (Fourteenth Amendment). But the court ruled that the First and Second Amendments were merely prohibitions applying to Congress and that, aside from those prohibitions, full jurisdiction over the rights to assemble and bear arms was left to each state. As for equal protection, the court held that the prosecution had not explicitly charged the defendants with acting for racial reasons. Moreover, the court enunciated a doctrine that would shape constitutional law ever after: the guarantee of equal protection applies only against the actions of states, not against anything private individuals might do.

The Civil Rights Act of 1870 also made it a criminal offense for election officials to refuse "to give to all citizens of the United States ... equal opportunity to ... become qualified to vote, without distinction of race or color" (section 2). Even though Congress enacted the law under the authority of the 15th Amendment, the constitutionality of the act was challenged in U.S. v. Reese (1876).

The case involved a Black man, William Garner, who was prevented from voting by state officials, even though he offered to pay the required poll tax and was otherwise qualified to vote. The official charged with receiving the tax payment refused to do so, and other officials thereupon refused to permit Garner to vote. The officials who prevented Garner from voting were charged for violating the 1870 law. The officials, in turn, argued that the law was unconstitutional.

The court noted that the specific sections of the act under which the charges were brought failed to expressly specify that it was only the race-based denial of the right to vote that was made a crime. The court held that this lack of specificity was fatal to the criminal charges, because everyone should be able to know for sure whether or not his conduct amounts to a crime. Additionally, the court held that key sections of the law exceeded the authority granted Congress by the 15th Amendment, because they did not expressly concern the interference with the right to vote based on race. But the court had chosen to overlook the plain fact that a central purpose of the law as a whole was to prohibit the denial of the right to vote on account of race.

The Civil Rights Act of 1875 aimed to protect the rights of Black Americans by banning discrimination based on race by privately-owned inns, hotels, theaters, and transportation companies. The act was a response to pervasive racial discrimination that limited the opportunity of Blacks to avail themselves of the services offered by those businesses to the general public.

However, in the Civil Rights Cases (1883), the Supreme Court struck down the act as unconstitutional. The court held that Congress had exceeded its lawful authority in enacting the legislation. Following the reasoning in Cruikshank, the court ruled that Congress was empowered, under the 14th Amendment, to ban racial discrimination by state governments but not by privately-owned companies. Moreover, access to the services of companies that do business with the general public was not a civil right, in the view of the court, but a mere "social right" (22), akin to the right to decide whom to invite to a dinner party, and the denial of such access did not violate the 13th Amendment because it was not among the essential elements of slavery.

Additionally, the court suggested that the 1875 law provided special treatment for Blacks and that such treatment was unwarranted. The court wrote, "When a man has emerged from slavery, and by the aid of beneficent legislation has shaken off the inseparable concomitants of that state, there must be some stage … when he takes the rank of a mere citizen, and ceases to be the special favorite of the laws (25).

A lone dissent in the case was authored by Justice Harlan, who contended that the court's understanding of the 13th and 14th Amendments was "entirely too narrow and artificial," with the result that "the substance and spirit of [those] amendments … have been sacrificed" (26). The purpose behind the 13th Amendment, Harlan argued, was not simply to do away with the legal ownership of Blacks but also to eliminate all laws and practices that forced upon Blacks a degraded and servile social status. He explained that, "since [slavery] rested wholly upon the inferiority, as a race, of those held in bondage, their freedom necessarily involved immunity from, and protection against, all discrimination against them, because of their race, in respect of such civil rights as belong to freemen of other races" (36). Accordingly, Harlan construed the amendment as empowering Congress to eradicate any law or practice that played a role in reducing Blacks to a position of comprehensive subordination to Whites.

In Harlan's view, a person who is denied access to public transportation on account of his race "is not only branded as one inferior and infected, but, in the competitions of life, is robbed of some of the most necessary means of existence; and all this solely because they belong to a particular race which the nation has liberated. The thirteenth amendment alone obliterated [this] race line" (40).

Turning to the 14th Amendment, Harlan rejected the idea that it never applied to privately-owned companies. He pointed out that the businesses to which the 1875 law applied were not fully private organizations but rather exercised special public functions regulated by the government, and so the acts of these businesses were subject to the 14th Amendment's requirement of equal protection. The requirement entailed, in Harlan's view, that "in respect of [civil] rights, there shall be no discrimination by the State, or ... [by] corporations exercising public functions ... against any citizen because of his race" (48).

Harlan insisted that the rights protected by the act were not mere social rights and did not regulate relationships such as those between friends or among members of private clubs. Rather, they were basic legal rights of citizenship, protected by the 14th Amendment. Accordingly, Harlan wrote, "The right ... of a colored citizen to use ... a public highway upon the same terms as are permitted to white citizens is no more a social right than his right, under the law, to use the public streets ... or a public market ..., or his right to sit in a public building with others, of whatever race" (59-60). Such rights were all essential to full and equal citizenship.

In his conclusion, Harlan rejected the court's suggestion that the act treated Black Americans as special favorites. Rather, the act sought nothing more than to provide to Black citizens the legal protections and powers that had already been granted to Whites. And, in Harlan's view, the Civil Rights Amendments demanded that there be no racial discrimination in matters pertaining to civil rights.

It took until the 1960's before the idea of a national prohibition on racial discrimination by privately-owned businesses was again placed on America's political agenda. In the meantime, the Jim Crow system of White supremacism had become entrenched in the South. The system deprived Blacks of their civil rights, flouting the legal guarantees of equality that had been enshrined in the Civil War Amendments and consigning Blacks to a subordinate and servile position in southern society. To mark Blacks as inferior, every southern state enacted a series of laws that required their segregation from Whites in schools, hospitals, cemeteries, public transportation, theaters, restaurants and many other places. In Plessy v. Ferguson (1896), the Supreme Court ruled that states were constitutionally permitted to legally require racial segregation in railway passenger cars and, by implication, in any other area of public life. The court thereby rejected Homer Plessy's 14th Amendment challenge to a Louisiana law that mandated "equal but separate accommodations" for Black and White passengers (540).

In Plessy, the court held that the state's law did not violate the 14th Amendment's guarantee of equal protection. Writing for the majority, Justice Brown held that the amendment "could not have been intended ... to enforce social as distinguished from political equality, or [to require] a commingling of the two races upon terms unsatisfactory to either" (544).

As for the idea that Louisiana's legislative act mandating racial segregation affixed a state-approved mark of inferiority on Blacks, Brown wrote, "We consider the underlying fallacy of [Plessy's] argument to consist in the assumption that the enforced separation of the two races stamps the colored race with a badge of inferiority. If this be so, it is not by reason of anything found in the act, but solely because the colored race chooses to put that construction upon it" (551).

The legal principle laid out in Plessy came to be called the doctrine of "separate-but-equal." The name was grossly misleading, because, notwithstanding the wording of the Louisiana law, the number and quality of the railway seats available for Blacks was not equal to those available to Whites. And across the Jim Crow South, the same was true of segregated schools, hospitals, theaters and so on. The name "separate-but-equal" was a blatant piece of hypocrisy that functioned to divert attention from the otherwise obvious fact that state-enforced racial segregation under Jim Crow violated the constitutionally-guaranteed civil rights of American Blacks.

Writing again in lone dissent, Justice Harlan pointed out that state laws requiring racial segregation "proceed on the ground that colored citizens are so inferior and degraded that they cannot be allowed to sit in public coaches occupied by white citizens" (560). Such laws thereby violated the Constitution, which he declared to be "color-blind" (559). The eyes of the court majority saw matters differently, but only by obtusely denying that state-mandated racial segregation in the South meant the official affirmation of White supremacy.

The early decades of the 20th century witnessed a continuation of unrestrained White attacks throughout the South on the persons and property of Blacks. Whites perpetrated violence against Blacks with impunity, as the violence was an important way by which Whites demonstrated and maintained their supremacy. Anti-lynching legislation was introduced into Congress in 1918, because states refused to prosecute the White perpetrators and local law enforcement officials were often complicit in the murders. But such legislation was not enacted, despite repeated efforts, and to this day Congress has failed to pass it.

In addition to the violence and severe discrimination to which Blacks under Jim Crow were subjected, their voting rights were flagrantly and pervasively denied by Southern states, while the U.S. Supreme Court refused to side with Blacks who sought the franchise. Perhaps it is unsurprising, then, that, during the 1920's, the radical Black nationalist Marcus Garvey was able to develop a substantial following for his movement, which urged Blacks to emigrate to Africa to escape the entrenched racism of Whites. Analogous to Theodor Herzl's conviction that anti-Semitism made equal citizenship for Jews impossible anywhere but in a Jewish state (see Chapter Five, section III), Garvey held that, due to irremediable anti-Black racism, American Blacks needed their own nation for their rights to be protected. Indeed, Garvey's movement was sometimes called "Black Zionism." But the movement dissipated after he was convicted of mail fraud and then deported upon his release from prison, and American Blacks would not again support in large numbers the idea of emigration as a solution to their oppression.

IV. The Long Civil Rights Movement

Jim Crow persisted through two World Wars and well-more than half a century of American history. Thousands of Blacks were lynched, as Whites ensured their social, political and legal dominance through widespread terror and the massive disenfranchisement of Black citizens. The Ku Klux Klan, which had been crushed during Reconstruction by federal military power, gained broad popularity after its rebirth in 1915. In a rewriting of history meant to assist the revival of the group, the original Klan was portrayed by White media not as a group of terrorists targeting innocent Blacks who might exercise their legal rights, but as heroes defending civilization against the onslaught of ignorant freedmen and their corrupt White allies. It would not be until the late 1960's that Jim Crow was dismantled and the Klan's reign of terror ended. And it would require a mass movement of American Blacks, risking their limbs, lives and livelihoods.

The conventional narrative of the Civil Rights Movement marks it as occurring over a bit more than a decade, from the mid-1950's to the late-1960's. Recent scholarship has challenged the conventional view, holding instead that there was a "long civil rights movement." On one prominent version of this newer picture, the beginnings of the movement were in the 1930's, when activists sought to promote economic justice for Blacks but also for working-class Whites, and its conclusion did not come about until the 1970's. Thus, the historian Jacquelyn Hall writes that the first phase of the Civil Rights Movement aimed at eliminating the stark economic inequalities of American society and reached its high-point in the 1940's as a broad-based and cross-racial coalition (2005).

A key episode in the long movement occurred in 1941 and revolved around the plan of Black labor leader A. Phillip Randolph to hold a mass march on Washington D.C., protesting the exclusion of Blacks from jobs in defense industries. Anxious to avoid the embarrassment such a demonstration would cause him, President Roosevelt agreed to sign an executive order obligating all defense contractors to refrain from employment discrimination on the basis of race. The order also required all federal training programs for jobs in the defense industry to be administered without such discrimination (E.O. 8802). The protest march was averted.

The war was fought to defend democracy against its fascist enemies. But American democracy was deeply racist, and Black veterans found that their service to the country did not mitigate the nation's racism. After the war, Whites continued to deny Blacks their civil rights, and Jim Crow remained alive and well.

In 1954, the Supreme Court finally decided to make a clean break with its "separate but equal" doctrine. The legal road to the decision was paved by a series of cases involving public graduate and professional schools. The court had ruled that the facilities at the Black schools were inferior to those at the corresponding White schools and so violated the constitutional guarantee of equal protection. The nation's oldest civil rights organization, the National Association for the Advancement of Colored People (NAACP), had brought the cases as part of a plan developed by the Black lawyer Charles H. Houston to undermine White support for Jim Crow by requiring states to pay the substantial costs involved in maintaining genuinely equal facilities for Blacks. The NAACP knew that cases involving the schooling of children would be much more controversial legally and politically than those involving graduate students and so held off on bringing those cases until favorable legal precedents had been set in the graduate and professional school cases.

Linda Brown was a Black child who had been excluded due to her race from the White public school near her home and forced to attend a more distant Black school. Her exclusion from the White school was authorized by state law. Brown's parents sued to enable her to attend the White school, but the lower federal court ruled against them, finding that the Black and White schools had "substantially equal facilities," including "buildings, curricula, qualifications and salaries of teachers, and other 'tangible' factors" (Brown v. Board of Education: 492). The Brown's then appealed to the Supreme Court.

Writing for a unanimous court, Chief Justice Earl Warren reversed the lower court. He noted that education was critically important for success in life and that offering an education to all citizens was among the most important functions of state and local governments. Accordingly, the court held that the 14th Amendment required states to offer equal educational opportunities for all their citizens.

Warren wrote that the key question in the case was, "Does segregation of children in public schools solely on the basis of race, even though the ... 'tangible' factors may be equal, deprive the children of the minority group of equal educational opportunities?" His answer for the court: "We believe that it does" (493).

Warren proceeded to explain the intangible factors at work. Citing the lower court and invoking several recent psychological studies, including one by the Black social psychologist Kenneth Clark, Warren affirmed that the "[s]egregation of white and colored children in public schools has a detrimental effect upon the colored children" and that "[t]he impact is greater when [segregation] has the sanction of the law, for the policy of separating the races is usually interpreted as denoting the inferiority of the negro group" (494). He added, "Any language in Plessy v. Ferguson contrary to this finding is rejected" (494-95).

Warren then announced the court's new interpretation of the 14th Amendment: "We conclude that, in the field of public education, the doctrine of 'separate but equal' has no place. Separate educational facilities are inherently unequal" (495). And so the court held that individuals had a constitutional right not to be excluded from any public school on account of their race.

The court's ruling was denounced by Southerners as an egregious instance of judicial tyranny. The "Declaration of Constitutional Principles," more popularly known as the "southern Manifesto" and signed by the majority of Southern members of Congress, proclaimed that the court's decision was an exercise of naked, lawless power. Some liberal legal theorists also had their doubts about the legal soundness of the court's reasoning, suggesting that there was no neutral principle of constitutional law that could justify the decision (Wechsler 1959). And there were Black critics. The author Zora Neale Hurston declared that the ruling was insulting to Blacks and an affront to their self-respect, because it rested on the racist belief that "there is no greater delight to Negroes than physical association with whites" (1955). And if Black schools had adequate resources, then, in her view, there would be no need for Blacks to go to school with Whites.

Moreover, the opinion in Brown continues to draw fire from prominent Blacks. The historian Ibram Kendi recently wrote, "Warren essentially offered a racist opinion in this landmark case: separate Black educational facilities were inherently unequal and inferior because Black students were not being exposed to White students" (2016: 362). However, like Hurston's view, Kendi's reading of the opinion is tendentious. Warren's claim about the inherent inferiority of Black schools was about the social meaning of racial separation in the context of America's history of anti-Black racism. His point was that Black children understood that their separation was a badge of inferiority affixed to them by White society and that such an understanding posed an impediment that unfairly denied to them equal educational opportunity. Warren was rejecting the declaration in Plessy that, if the enforced separation of Whites and Blacks stamped the latter with a badge of inferiority, it was only because

Blacks interpreted the separation in that way. *Contra* Hurston and Kendi, the rejection of such a declaration is hardly insulting or racist.

V. The Classic Period of the Movement

The time from 1955 to 1968 was a decisive one in the struggle of American Blacks for the recognition and protection of their civil rights. The time has been called the "classic period" of the Civil Rights Movement. During this period, the mainstream civil rights organizations, such as the NAACP, led by Roy Wilkins, and the Southern Christian Leadership Conference (SCLC), headed by Martin Luther King, Jr., were committed to the goals of a) racial integration in all the major spheres of American life, including education, employment, housing, public facilities, and business and b) the enfranchisement of southern Blacks. To achieve these goals, the mainstream groups undertook nonviolent protests, litigation, and the formation of alliances with northern Whites. The groups also regarded the federal government as indispensable for the achievement of its goals and so sought to work with, and put pressure on, the President and leaders of Congress to advance those goals through executive action and legislation.

The mainstream civil rights leaders regarded their program as the only feasible way to bring about

American society's recognition and protection of the rights of Blacks. Their organizations relied substantially on financial assistance from northern Whites, particularly when southern authorities sought to bankrupt the organizations through a barrage of lawsuits and mass arrests of demonstrators, who needed cash to be bailed out of jail. Any use or threat of violence by the movement would alienate the mainstream's White allies in the North. Violence would also make it politically impossible for the President and Congress to help advance the goals of the movement. Moreover, mainstream leaders regarded the use of violence as morally problematic: morality demanded that Blacks appeal to the conscience of Whites, persuading them that justice required Black freedom and equality. And violence would undercut any hope of racial integration, as it would destroy any prospect that Whites would be willing to accept Blacks into their neighborhoods, businesses, and other domains of life.

The mainstream positions were most forcefully presented and defended by King, in his many speeches and writings. He declared, "The Negroes' goal is freedom" and explained, "Our position depends upon a lot more than political power … It depends upon our ability to marshal moral power as well" (1986: 111 and 59). In King's view, nonviolent protesters were using their "very bodies as a means of laying [their] case before the conscience of the local and the national community" (291). By protesting nonviolently, the Black person showed the morally required respect for his opponent, while the discipline involved in such protesting had given the Black protester a new and morally elevated image of himself, an image not warped by the countless messages from the White world of his racial inferiority. In King's judgment, integration was an ethical demand, based on the equal and intrinsic worth of all persons and on the value of freedom. And the reciprocal relations between means and ends entailed that the goal of integration required nonviolent means: "We want to share in the American economy, the housing market, the educational system and the social opportunities. The goal itself indicates that a social change in America must be nonviolent" (58). Moreover, the resort to violence by Blacks must reckon with "the possible casualties to a minority population confronting a well-armed, wealthy majority with a fanatical right wing that is capable of exterminating the entire black population." Accordingly, King held that "for practical as well as moral reasons, nonviolence offers the only road to freedom for my people" (55).

The mainstream organizations and leaders dominated the Black struggle for civil rights until the mid-1960's, when a number of militant Black organizations and leaders emerged to challenge the mainstream as misguided and ineffectual. Their views were foreshadowed in some respects by Malcolm X, who had become by the late 1950's the principal public face of the religious organization, the Nation of Islam, led by Elijah Muhammad. The Nation preached racial separatism, regarding Whites as a race of devils who would be destroyed by the avenging hand of Allah. In the Nation's view, Blacks needed to cultivate strict moral discipline and rely solely on their own community. Additionally, Muhammad decreed that politics were to be avoided and that the members of the group eschew any involvement in the Civil Rights Movement, as the fate of Blacks was in the hands of Allah and not of mere humans.

While still a member of the Nation, Malcolm regularly denounced mainstream leaders, including Martin Luther King, as stooges of the White man and as "Uncle Toms." He ridiculed the failure of protestors to strike back when they were attacked by vigilantes and police, and he rejected the idea that any Whites could be counted on to fight against the oppression of Blacks.

After leaving the Nation of Islam, Malcolm publicly modified some, but not all, of his ideas. He advocated political action by Blacks, first and foremost, action to secure the franchise. He moderated his criticisms of mainstream Black leaders. He gave up the notion that Whites were a race of devils, acknowledging that some Whites might assist the Black struggle but only by working in their own, White organizations to change the racist mentality of their fellow Whites. And he still rejected the mainstream's firm commitment to nonviolence, its willingness to accept Whites in its organizations, its appeals to the federal government for the protection of Black rights, and its goal of racial integration.

1. Malcolm X waiting for a press conference to begin on March 26, 1964.

Speaking to a Black audience in New York, Malcolm declared, "You, today, are in the hands of a government of segregationists." He argued, "If the United States government doesn't want you and me to get rifles, then take the rifles away from those racists … If they don't want you and me to get violent, then stop the racists from being violent. Don't teach us on violence while those crackers are violent. Those days are over" (1964a). And implicitly addressing King and the mainstream, Malcolm said that "you think that integration will get you freedom; I think that separation will get me freedom" (1964b).

Malcolm formed several organizations after his break with the Nation of Islam, but none was successful in attracting much support or affecting the course of the movement for Black freedom. In the years after his assassination in 1965, though, militant Blacks influenced by Malcolm's ideas took leadership roles in existing organizations that had previously been part of the mainstream or formed new organizations of their own. These militants created the Black Power Movement, which, in the eyes of many observers, marked the end of the Civil Rights Movement. The premises of these militant leaders and groups were that the mainstream organizations had utterly failed to liberate Blacks from their oppression, that the failure reflected the bankruptcy of mainstream ideas, and that anti-Black racism and White supremacy still reigned in America. Before turning to Black Power, let us examine a bit more of the classic period of the Civil Rights Movement and the most important pieces of legislation to come out of it.

VI. Southern Resistance and the National Government

During the classic period, the leaders of the mainstream organizations were disappointed time and again by the federal government. President Eisenhower was not sympathetic to the civil rights cause, and he was extremely reluctant to use his powers to ensure that the constitutional rights of Blacks in the South were protected. Only in the egregious case of Little Rock, Arkansas, where desegregation orders by a federal court were flagrantly defied, did Eisenhower send federal troops to ensure that a handful of Black schoolgirls could attend the previously all-White Central High School. President Kennedy proved to be only a little better. During his administration, activists seeking to register Blacks to vote in the South were subjected to violence by White supremacists, who acted with impunity. Despite the clear violations of the 15th Amendment, the President and his brother, Attorney General Robert Kennedy, disingenuously claimed that there was no legal basis for federal intervention. Only when Whites rioted to prevent the court-ordered enrollment of one lone Black person, James Meredith, at the previously all-White University of Mississippi, did President Kennedy send in federal troops to ensure Meredith's enrollment. Meredith succeeded in enrolling, but most public schools and universities across the deep South remained segregated, notwithstanding the decision in Brown v. Board of Education and a host of federal court rulings against racial segregation. By the 1963-64 school year, only 1.2% of Black children in the South attended school with Whites, the result of pervasive defiance by southern Whites of federal court orders (Rosenberg 1993: 50).

Southern resistance to the dismantling of Jim Crow combined raw violence with the strategic deployment of local and state law. Oftentimes, local and state law enforcement officials perpetrated the violence. Despite scores of killings of civil rights activists and bombings of their homes and offices, virtually no one was convicted of those crimes. Instead, the activists were routinely prosecuted and convicted on trumped-up charges when they peacefully protested, sought to register Black voters, and otherwise exercised their constitutional rights. The law was used by officials as an instrument of arbitrary White power, and so it was deployed or ignored, as convenience dictated (in the U.S., criminal law is largely a matter of state, rather than federal, law).

Moreover, there was a symbiotic relationship between the use of the law and the criminal tactics of White segregationists. Between 1956 and 1960 alone, southern legislatures enacted more than 200 laws designed to intimidate the members of civil rights organizations such as the NAACP and to bankrupt the groups (Lewis: 92). These laws often worked in tandem with criminal violence against civil rights activists. For example, an Alabama law demanded that the NAACP hand over to state officials its list of members; the purpose was to threaten the members with public exposure, making them easy targets of violent White supremacist groups like the KKK. Membership in the state's chapter of the NAACP shriveled as a result, and between 1956 and 1964, the organization had to shut down operations in Alabama.

Against fierce southern opposition, three major pieces of national legislation were enacted during the classic period of the Civil Rights Movement. The first was the Civil Rights Act of 1964, which provided that "[a]ll persons shall be entitled to the full and equal enjoyment of the goods, services, [and] facilities ... of any place of public accommodation ... without discrimination or segregation on the ground of race, color, religion, or national origin" (Title II). Such places included hotels, motels, restaurants, and entertainment venues.

Additionally, the act declared, "It shall be an unlawful employment practice for an employer to fail or refuse to hire or to discharge any individual ... because of such individual's race, color, religion, sex, or national origin" (Title VII), and that no program or activity receiving federal funds was permitted to exclude persons on account of race (Title VI).

In Heart of Atlanta Motel v. U.S. (1964), the Supreme Court upheld the constitutionality of the act. The court ruled that Congress's authority to regulate interstate commerce, granted by Article I of the Constitution, encompassed the power to prohibit racial discrimination by privately-owned businesses that served the public. As long as a business had some connection to interstate commerce, Congress had the power to forbid the business from discriminating on the basis of race.

The decision in the Civil Rights Cases (1883), according to the court, was "inapposite and without precedential value" (Heart of Atlanta: 250), because those cases did not involve interstate commerce. The court pointed out that the 1964 act was not only about commerce, because the law also addressed what Congress regarded as a moral problem. But the court contended that, as long as Congress's aim was to remove a hindrance to interstate commerce, the fact that the hindrance was also deemed a moral wrong did not place the law beyond the power of Congress to enact.

The 1964 law proved to be an important instrument in the dismantling of Jim Crow. Title VI was especially important in desegregating public schools when Congress began the next year to offer to states large amounts of money to help fund education. Many southern states chose to desegregate rather than forgo the money, thus vindicating in an unexpected way Charles

Houston's belief that financial incentives could be sufficiently powerful to undermine Jim Crow (see section IV above).

The Voting Rights Act of 1965 was the second major piece of legislation to come out of the classic period of the Civil Rights Movement. The law was enacted as a direct result of the famous five-day, 54-mile march of civil rights protestors from Selma, Alabama to the state capital of Montgomery. The march was initially blocked by the violence of police and vigilantes. The violence was captured by TV cameras and photographed by journalists, and it created a powerful national and international backlash against the segregationist cause.

The 1965 law turned out to be the most effective piece of civil rights legislation in American history. Within a few years, the number of Blacks registered to vote in the deep South increased exponentially. In 1964, 6.7% of voting-age Blacks were registered in Mississippi and 23% in Alabama, far lower than the White registration rates. But by 1970, the Black-White gap had almost disappeared, with Black registration reaching 67% and 64% in those two states, respectively. Other states in the region that had been less egregious in denying Blacks the right to vote still saw substantial increases in Black registration: Louisiana went from 32% to 62%, Georgia from 44% to 64%, and South Carolina from 39% to 57% (Carmines and Huckfeldt: 1992: 128).

This increase in Black voter registration, in turn, led to a large increase in the number of Black elected officials, especially at the local level, and those officials were able to secure better access to basic public services like paved roads and sanitation for Black communities.

Essential to the effectiveness of the Voting Rights Act were provisions that placed substantial limits on the power of states to regulate voting. One section of the act provided for the appointment of federal officials to register voters, thereby bypassing the racially discriminatory actions that local registrars had undertaken to disenfranchise Blacks. Another provision contained a statistical criterion for picking out jurisdictions with a history of voter suppression and prohibited those jurisdictions from using various registration requirements that southern states had long employed in a racially discriminatory manner. The banned requirements included literacy tests, which often involved questions about recondite matters of state law, and good character requirements, which called for applicants to have a respected member of the (White) community attest to their character. Yet another provision of the act required jurisdictions with a history of suppression to submit to the federal government for approval any changes that they wished to make in their voting systems. The changes would be approved only if they did not have the purpose or effect of abridging or denying the right to vote on account of race. Because southern states had a record of changing their systems in creative ways to prevent Black voting, this provision of the law sought to block any newly invented ploys for disenfranchising Blacks.

More than a few conservative political commentators at the time attacked the Voting Rights Act as a violation of state's rights and of the federalist system established by the Constitution in which political powers were divided between the national and state levels. Writing in the pages of the country's most prominent conservative journal, *The National Review*, James J. Kilpatrick characterized the legislation as "a wrecking ball [striking] at the very foundations of American federalism" (1965: 319). Kilpatrick conceded that southern states had defied the 15th Amendment but went on to lay out "extenuating circumstances." He explained, "Over most of this century, the great bulk of Southern Negroes have been genuinely unqualified for the franchise. They emerged illiterate from slavery; they remained for generations, metaphorically, under the age of twenty-one. To this day, such is the apathetic state of rural politics in the South, the problem is not merely that registrars deny, but that Negroes seldom ask. The evidence would show this." Moreover, in those southern jurisdictions with black majorities, he asserted, it had been Whites who had maintained the functions of government: "To have yielded political control of these functions to a mass of relatively uneducated Negro voters, easily led, unequipped for public administration, would have meant total disintegration of the whole establishment" (319). In Kilpatrick's view, the disenfranchisement of Blacks was a "limited evil" that did not need the heavy machinery of the Voting Rights Act to eliminate (322).

Contrary to Kilpatrick's speculations about the calamitous consequences of allowing "a mass of relatively uneducated Negro voters" to exert political power, the exponential increases in Black voter registration that occurred in the wake of the Voting Rights Act did not lead to the disintegration of public administration. What it led to were substantial improvements in the public services provided to Black neighborhoods and regions: paved roads, sewage treatment facilities, and other public goods that had been formerly reserved for Whites were now extended to Blacks. And the evidence would have shown that, during much of the reign of Jim Crow, Blacks had seldom asked for the vote because they knew from experience that doing so would have placed them in grave danger of physical and economic retaliation. Even so, by the 1960's, Blacks were frequently demanding the franchise, their efforts culminating in the Selma to Montgomery march.

The concern with protecting American federalism above all else was not limited to conservatives. During its three years in power, the Kennedy administration repeatedly invoked federalism to justify its spotty record in protecting the civil rights of Blacks. The administration shared one crucial intellectual failure with the conservative critics of the Civil Rights Movement: they all failed to come to grips with the fact that, under Jim Crow, the rule of law did not exist for Blacks. Jim Crow was a system of racial terror in which the legal rights of Blacks counted for nothing. It was a system that reflected Chief Justice Taney's declaration in the Dred Scott case that Blacks had no rights that Whites were bound to respect. Southern states had used the political powers that they possessed under the Constitution to brazenly flout the rule of law and trample on the constitutional rights of Blacks. Allowing those states to continue their defiance of the Constitution by appealing to the Constitution was a legal and practical contradiction that made a mockery of the nation's highest law. For the sake of the Constitution, the only option was for the national government to impose on southern states restrictions reasonably calculated to vindicate the rights of Blacks, even if those restrictions would have been unconstitutional had they been imposed on states that had not used their powers in the egregious manner that southern states had in fact done.

The Civil Rights Act of 1968, more popularly known as the "Fair Housing Act," was the final major piece of civil rights legislation in the classic period of the movement. It prohibited discrimination based on race in the sale, rental or financing of housing. In an effort to combat the racial segregation of neighborhoods, the law also prohibited real estate agents from steering home buyers only to areas already populated by persons of the same race as the buyers.

Housing discrimination and the residential segregation connected to it were deeply embedded in American society, and, for decades, the federal government pursued policies that explicitly supported segregated housing. The government provided mortgage insurance to White homebuyers who were purchasing homes in White areas but, in a practice known as "redlining," refused to provide insurance to anyone seeking a home in areas where Blacks were concentrated. A federal manual instructed appraisers to lower their estimates of the values of homes in racially integrated and Black neighborhoods. Thus, the federal government not only reinforced residential segregation but also planted the seeds for the enormous growth in the Black-White gap in wealth, because, during the period after World War II, owning a home came to be the primary source of wealth for many Americans. Since the 1980's, the median wealth of Whites has been approximately ten times that of Blacks.

If the Voting Rights Act of 1965 had proved to be a major success, the Fair Housing Act was largely a failure. Despite the provisions of the law, real estate agents continued to practice discrimination on a widespread basis. Banks offered to Blacks less favorable terms on mortgage loans than those offered to Whites. And extreme residential segregation persisted through the ensuing decades. The act had failed to give enforcement powers to the federal agency that oversaw matters of housing, the Department of Housing and Urban Development, instead authorizing lawsuits by individual plaintiffs against landlords, mortgage brokers and real estate agents. The history of voting rights showed that systemic racial discrimination could not be effectively fought with lawsuits by individual private parties but rather required vigorous federal enforcement of antidiscrimination laws.

VII. Black Power and Urban Insurrection: The End of the Civil Rights Movement?

According to the conventional account, the Civil Rights Movement ended in 1968. When Google is queried 'When was the Civil Rights Movement?', the answer that comes back is '1954-1968', with the answer posted against a white background that looks eerily like a tombstone. The assassination of Martin Luther King and the subsequent riots in Black communities across the country are said to have brought the movement to its conclusion. The Fair Housing Act, which was passed just days after the assassination and in response to it and the riots that followed, is often regarded as the movement's final, posthumous achievement.

By 1968, the widespread perception among Whites was that Black Americans had largely shifted their commitments from the nonviolent strategy and integrationist goals of King and the civil rights mainstream to the more militant approach taken by Black Power advocates. The path to that perception was paved by the riots that took place in the Black sections of many American cities, starting in 1964 and reaching a crescendo in the wake of King's assassination, when violence broke out in more than 100 places, and by the emerging prominence of militant leaders like Stokely Carmichael (Kwame Ture) and Huey Newton and organizations like the Black Panther Party.

It was both ironic and understandable that some Blacks responded with violence to the violence that killed the country's most visible apostle of nonviolence. An affirmation of King's life and values was hardly compatible with rioting. But King represented more than a commitment to nonviolence. He was the most prominent and celebrated Black American, and, at an abstract level, he represented Black freedom to both Blacks and Whites, quite apart from his strategy for achieving freedom or even from his integrationist view of what Black freedom would involve. His assassination was seen by many Blacks as an emphatic repudiation by White America of the Black aspiration for freedom.

Rioting was the reply of many rightly enraged Blacks to that repudiation.

In any event, the Black militants of the 1960's rejected nonviolence and integration. Ture, who had introduced the term 'black power' in 1966, and Charles Hamilton wrote that "black people in this country form a colony, and it is not in the interest of the colonial power to liberate them" (1967/1992: 5). Like many Black militants of the era, they saw the efforts of American Blacks to achieve freedom as "closely related to liberation struggles around the world" (xix). Specifically, "Black and colored people are saying in a clear voice that they intend to determine for themselves the kinds of political, social, and economic systems they will live under" (179). Ture and Hamilton noted that, for American Blacks, the intention to achieve collective self-determination did not mean the creation of a separate and sovereign Black country; rather it meant that Blacks should form their own political parties and community-based organizations to control local institutions and gain "full participation in the decision-making processes affecting the lives of black people" (47).

Ture and Hamilton also condemned the integrationist efforts of the civil rights mainstream. They wrote that "while colorblindness *may* be a sound goal ultimately, we must realize that race is an overwhelming fact of life in this historical period" (1967/1992: 54; emphasis in original). Their point was that, contrary to the mainstream view, integration should not be a goal that guides action in the current era. As an action-guiding goal, integration was "based on the assumption that there is nothing of value in the black community" and constituted "a subterfuge for the maintenance of white supremacy," according to Ture and Hamilton (53 and 54). And alluding to Brown v. Board of Education, they wrote, "The goal is not to take black children out of the black community and expose them to white middle-class values; the goal is to build and strengthen the black community." In their view, "integration, as traditionally conceived, would abolish the black community" by dispersing Blacks into a sea of White institutions and neighborhoods. In the process, the cultural integrity and racial pride of the Black community would be destroyed.

The mainstream reliance on legislation was also criticized as ineffective by Black militants. They saw no improvement resulting from the new civil rights legislation in the lives of Blacks. Thus, Ture and Hamilton wrote, "Congress passed civil rights law after civil rights law, only to have them effectively nullified by deliberately weak enforcement" (1967/1992: 51).

The Black Panther Party became the most prominent of the militant groups of the late 1960's and early 70's. The Panthers publicly displayed their weapons and organized patrols to follow the police and deter brutality against the residents of Black neighborhoods. One wing of the group advocated immediate, violent revolution, while another delivered meals and other social services to Black neighborhoods. The Panthers were involved in a number of lethal confrontations with the police. The report of an unofficial commission of inquiry jointly headed by the leader of the NAACP and a former U.S. Attorney General examined a notorious police raid in Chicago that resulted in the killing of state party leaders and concluded that the police who had planned and carried out the raid "acted with wanton disregard of human life and the legal rights of American citizens" (Commission of Inquiry 1973: viii). The commission also found that there was probable cause to believe that one of the Panthers, Fred Hampton, was murdered by the police. It was not the only case in which credible charges were made that police had murdered members of the party.

Additionally, the FBI engaged in secretive, unlawful activities to discredit and destroy the party, employing agent provocateurs and illegal wiretaps. These efforts by the bureau were a continuation of the campaign it had previously conducted to ruin the reputation of Martin Luther King and undermine the Civil Rights Movement, ostensibly because the mainstream organizations were infiltrated by Communists under the control of the Soviet Union, a charge supported by only the flimsiest of evidence but promoted by the FBI because its Director, J. Edgar Hoover, stood against Black equality. The charge of Communist infiltration was repeatedly made in public by opponents of the movement and was meant to send the message that its supporters were not loyal Americans. And as we will see in the next chapter with Jewish emancipation, the tactic of casting doubt on the political loyalty of the members of subordinated groups is an old tactic of those seeking to keep those persons in their place.

At the same time, an important strand of thinking among the Panthers and other Black militants held that American capitalism and White supremacy were joined at the hip and needed to be destroyed together. Accordingly, many Black activists advocated socialism or communism, although they were certainly not operating under Soviet direction. Huey Newton, co-founder of the Panthers, said that his brand of revolutionary Black nationalism was committed to socialism. And Angela Davis, the most prominent female Black militant, was a member of both the Panthers and an all-Black faction of the U.S. Communist Party.

In their condemnation of capitalism, Newton, Davis and other militants were continuing a line of thinking among American Black activists and intellectuals that went back to the 1920's, when the Communist Party-USA was the only political party in the country that advocated racial equality and denounced Jim Crow. The Black thinker Harry Haywood had been a party member and, during the 1930's, he had exercised substantial influence on the party's analysis of racial oppression in the U.S. (he was expelled from the party in the late 1950's). Haywood had described American Blacks as constituting a nation and had characterized the region across the South where they formed a majority (the so-called "Black Belt") as "a kind of 'internal colony' of American imperialism" (1948: 146). He had written that "the right and exercise of self-determination is the inherent goal of the Negro struggle for national liberation" (162). The right would be initially exercised as a kind of regional autonomy in the Black Belt. But Haywood believed that eventually the Black majority in that region would decide whether or not to form its own sovereign state.

By the 1950's, migration to the North had rendered obsolete Haywood's anticipation of regional autonomy for Blacks in the Black Belt. Still, during the 1960's, many militant Blacks, including Newton and Ture, contended that Black communities were internal colonies that authorities and businesses oppressed and exploited. And that contention would help fuel the call of the Panthers and other militants for Black community self-determination.

The Black Power advocates of the 1960's and early 70's offered a radical alternative to the mainstream of the Civil Rights Movement, which they regarded as a failure based on mistaken ideas about the depth and breadth of anti-Black racism and flawed assumptions about the possibility of achieving equal rights for Blacks within the existing political and economic framework. There was much truth to their understanding of American society, as later years have borne out. Political and economic institutions have left a substantial proportion of American Blacks destitute and isolated in segregated inner-city neighborhoods. The income and wealth of Black households still lag far behind the figures for Whites. Blacks across the socioeconomic spectrum are subject to police harassment and brutality on account of their race. And anti-Black prejudice and discrimination remain widespread.

The persisting social, political, and economic inequality of Blacks in America means that, notwithstanding their equality of rights under the law, their civil rights are less secure than those of Whites. For that reason, the promise of the Civil Rights Amendments is still unfulfilled, and Blacks remain less than equal citizens. It is unsurprising, then, that the organized efforts of American Blacks and their White allies to achieve racial equality have not ceased. Among the efforts are the protests against police brutality by Black Lives Matter and the local groups seeking to hold officers accountable for the unjustifiable killing of Blacks (see Chapter Seven, section IV). The pursuit of racial justice has also included efforts to bring an end to mass incarceration, which has had a disproportionate and devastating impact on Black families and communities, and to restore voting rights to felons, who are often disenfranchised by state laws. Those efforts and many more are a continuation of the Civil Rights Movement, pursuing its unfinished agenda.

2. Photograph of Dr. Martin Luther King Jr. addressing the crowd during the 1957 Prayer Pilgrimage for Freedom in Washington, D.C.

In his last presidential address to the SCLC, Martin Luther King said that "the movement must address itself to the question of restructuring the whole of American society" (1967/2004: 153). He was referring to an economic and political transformation that would eradicate poverty and embody a synthesis of the truths of capitalism and socialism. King saw his "Poor Peoples' campaign," which he embarked upon in the final year of his life, as a step toward that synthesis. It might seem that King was moving away from the Civil Rights Movement with the campaign and his calls for restructuring society. But he did not see things that way, and we shouldn't do so.

The 1963 March on Washington, where King gave his iconic "I Have A Dream Speech," was called by its organizers a march "for jobs and freedom" and involved a series of substantive economic demands, including "a massive federal program to train and place all unemployed workers —Negro and white— on meaningful and dignified jobs at a decent wage" and national minimum wage legislation that would "give all Americans a decent standard of living" (Ahmann et al. 1963). In the context of American capitalism, those were transformative demands, and mainstream civil rights activists drew no simple line between civil rights and economic claims that went beyond the rights recognized by existing market arrangements. They understood that, just as the distinction between civil and political rights was a false one, so was the distinction between civil rights and substantive economic rights. That understanding was shared by Black Power militants, however much they disagreed with mainstream organizations in their vision of the society to be brought about and the means to achieve it. Nonetheless, American society effectively turned its back on this point of agreement between the mainstream and the militants, as the years since the early 1970's brought a form of politics dominated by the neoliberal embrace of a version of capitalism in which large banks and corporations dictated the economic rules to a degree not seen since before the New Deal. The highly progressive economic demands of the mainstream organizations and leaders during the 1960's has been largely forgotten in the American remembrance of the Civil Rights Movement.

Chapter 5
Jewish Emancipation

I. Background

From the 12th through the 18th centuries, the Jews of Europe were not regarded as members of the societies in which they resided. They were not slaves, but they led a socially-precarious existence, lacking elementary rights enjoyed by their Christian neighbors. Jews had no right of residence and were repeatedly expelled from cities and even entire countries. Even when Jews were permitted to reside in a certain place, their numbers were often limited by the decree of the ruler, and, in many cities, they were permitted to live only in ghettos, walled-off neighborhoods accessible through a single gate that was locked from the outside at night. It was illegal for Jews to be outside of the ghetto after the gate was shut. Severe restrictions were also imposed on the occupations that they could pursue, largely limiting Jews to jobs that were menial or —like moneylending— morally tainted in the eyes of Christian society. Jews enjoyed some degree of liberty of worship, but their rituals and services were restricted to private homes and buildings whose Jewish identity was not visible from the public streets. Freedom of movement was restricted as was, in some places, the freedom to marry.

Hatred of Jews was widespread and by no means limited to the uneducated masses. In his essay, "On the Jews and Their Lies," Martin Luther recommended to Christian rulers that they burn down synagogues, seize all copies of the Talmud, and prohibit Jews from praying or uttering God's name in public. If those measures were not taken, Luther suggested, then Jews should "be driven from the country and be told to … move to … Jerusalem, where they may lie, curse, blaspheme, spit, murder, steal, rob, practice usury, mock, and engage in all such slanderous abominations as they do among us" (1543/1948: 52).

A century and a half later, the English philosopher John Locke took a view very different from Luther's, defending religious toleration for a range of groups that were subjected to continuing persecution. Locke argued that, in addition to Protestant dissenters from the Anglican Church, "neither *Pagan*, nor *Mahumetan*, nor *Jew*, ought to be excluded from the Civil Rights of the Commonwealth" (1689/1983: 54, emphases in original; Locke did not extend toleration to Roman Catholics on the ground that they were loyal to the Pope, not to their secular ruler). The jurisdiction of the state extended only to the concerns of this life and not to the salvation of souls. The state exceeded its jurisdiction if it denied equal rights to persons on the ground that their religious beliefs and practices posed a threat to the souls of their neighbors. However, it was not until a century after Locke that a political process began by which European Jews would eventually gain their civil rights.

Jewish emancipation was a complex collection of events and processes that played out across more than a hundred years. For Jews, emancipation involved a liberation from the impositions of Christian society but also the destruction of elements of their traditional culture. For that reason, Jewish emancipation vividly illustrates the conflict between civil rights and certain kinds of cultural formations.

Prior to emancipation, being Jewish was a comprehensive way of life that went well beyond adherence to particular beliefs about what was holy. That way of life was organized around Jewish law (halakhah), encompassing the 613 commandments that Moses was said to have written down in the

Torah and the various elaborations and glosses developed by leading rabbis and eventually written down in the Talmud. Jewish law regulated in detail the daily lives of Jews, so that virtually every activity had a sacred dimension, and the modern distinction between the secular and the sacred had no purchase within their way of life. And in the centuries prior to emancipation, Jewish communities in Europe were granted by Christian rulers a significant degree of autonomy to order their affairs according to how their local rabbis and leading laymen decided. The authority included the right to punish by fines and physically confine those Jews who violated the community norms and decisions. This community autonomy was granted, however, on the premise that Jews would accept their subordinate, marginal, and insecure position within Christendom.

The preservation of their community was of supreme importance for Jews, because the community was their only source of security in a profoundly hostile Christian world. The idea of an individual's right to deviate from community norms would have made no sense to them. And vital to community survival, in the eyes of Jews, was maintaining a secure link to their tradition. Importantly, traditional Jewish schooling did not incorporate the general study of science, literature, or philosophy but was limited to the sacred texts and the traditional elaborations and stories meant to convey the knowledge contained in those texts;

all other putative knowledge was thought to be worthless or dangerous. Additionally, tradition dictated that advanced education be given only to boys and consist of the intensive study of the Talmud.

Christian advocates of Jewish emancipation understood that the traditional Jewish way of life did not fit well with the modern state that had emerged in Europe by the 18th century. They pointed out that, for example, education in subjects like science would be needed for Jews to become citizens who contributed as much to the common good as did Christians. Accordingly, in the early 19th century, a number of states pursuing emancipationist policies required Jewish children to be schooled in secular subjects in addition to their Jewish studies. Secular education had, in fact, been advocated since the late 18th century by a growing number of reformist Jewish thinkers and leaders, who had been influenced by the ideas of the Enlightenment, with its affirmation of the power of human reason and science to dispel the darkness of age-old superstition and bring the light of knowledge to humankind.

Perhaps, the deepest tension between Jewish emancipation and traditional Jewish life in Europe stemmed from the uneasy relation between the individual and the community. Emancipation was a matter of gaining civil rights, and civil rights belonged to individuals; traditional Jewish life was not about individual rights but rather about the preservation of the practices of the community. Traditionalist Jews tended to look askance on emancipation, because they saw it as undermining communal solidarity. They were also convinced that Jews could not become integrated into society without turning their backs on Jewish law and custom. By contrast, Jews who advocated emancipation saw the emergence of the modern state and the rule of law as calling for a justifiable modification of traditional Jewish ways, so that Jews could gain civil rights and live as equal citizens under the law.

Although there were different ways in which Jewish life could have been adapted to the modern state, some modification in their traditional way of life was clearly necessary if Jews as individuals were to gain equal citizenship in such a state. Traditionalists and reformists both understood that emancipation was not completely compatible with traditional Jewish life.

II. The Beginnings of the Process

At the start of the process of Jewish emancipation in the late 18th century, the "enlightened" monarchs of central Europe such as the Habsburg Emperor Joseph II initiated a step-by-step policy in which new privileges were gradually extended to Jews. The idea was that Jews would have time and opportunity to improve themselves morally and thereby to show that they deserved equal legal status with Christians. This incrementalist approach rested, in part, on a premise that had been accepted in Christian Europe for centuries: Jews were morally corrupt, clannish, and especially prone to cheating Christians in commercial dealings and to perpetrating crimes against them. While Luther had seen the moral corruption of Jews as both extreme and inherent in the practice of Judaism, Joseph II thought that Jews should be given the opportunity to reform themselves morally and that legal equality should be approached in stages to ensure that the supposedly necessary moral regeneration had taken place.

The Prussian civil servant Christian Wilhelm von Dohm, however, published an essay in 1781 that argued (with some qualification) that the equal citizenship of Jews should be established immediately. Dohm wrote the essay at the suggestion of the philosopher Moses Mendelssohn, who was an observant Jew and believed that strict obedience to Jewish law was not incompatible with equal citizenship. Mendelssohn recognized that an argument for Jewish emancipation would carry more weight in the eyes of Christians if it were not coming from a Jew. Knowing that Dohm was sympathetic to emancipation, Mendelssohn asked him whether he would be willing to publish an essay defending it. Dohm's essay was highly progressive for the time, and although Mendelssohn had reservations about its argument, he described the work as excellent and Dohm as a friend of humankind.

Dohm accepted the idea that Jews were more morally corrupt than Christians, but, rather than attributing the corruption to something inherent to Judaism or Jews, he explained it as a consequence of the oppression that they had been living under for so long and advocated the granting of full and equal civil rights to Jews. Dohm agreed with Joseph II that Jews must undergo a moral regeneration to become good citizens but rejected Joseph's incrementalist approach, arguing that equal civil rights would lead to Jews becoming such citizens.

However, Dohm also believed that the moral regeneration would not happen overnight, and he was concerned about the access of Jews to public office. At the time, they were banned from holding office, on the ground that they lacked loyalty to the state where they resided and thought of their homeland as Palestine, to which they believed they would return and form a Jewish state when their Messiah arrived. Dohm wrote, "It seems ... that if [Jews] are granted all civil rights, they could not be excluded from applying for the honor to serve the government, and if they are found capable, to be employed by the state" (1781/2011: 31). But he quickly added that not many Jews of his generation would have the education needed to qualify for a position in government. And in most European countries, he explained, there were more than enough Christians who possessed the necessary skills. So Dohm proposed that Jews who showed special talents could get a job in a public position, but, as between a Jew and an equally qualified Christian, the Christian is to be preferred.

In the end, then, Dohm and Joseph II both thought that there was a "Jewish problem," i.e., both of them believed that there was something morally and politically deficient with Jews. They disagreed over how, and how quickly, the deficiencies could be remedied. Dohm's proposals involved large and immediate steps toward Jewish emancipation, by contrast with Joseph's relatively cautious edicts. But even Dohm's bold approach was hedged with qualifications, reflecting his view of the challenges to be overcome in extending civil rights to the members of a group that had been oppressed for centuries and had, in his view, adapted to its oppression in certain unfortunate ways.

Notice that there was an unexamined tension in Dohm's argument. He failed to acknowledge that the oppression of Jews by Christians was itself a form of corruptness. In light of the Christian mistreatment of Jews and the unjust advantages Christians thereby gained for themselves, it was far from clear that Christians were any less corrupt, and, as Mendelssohn would suggest, it was arguable that they were more so. But the unquestioned assumption of Christian society was that it was the Jews, not Christians, who were the problem.

Mendelssohn realized that the charge of Jewish corruption rested on an unduly narrow understanding of what counted as corruption, and so he was not entirely happy with Dohm's argument. But Mendelssohn's explicit target for criticism was Johann David Michaelis, an opponent of Jewish emancipation who was a prominent Christian scholar of ancient Palestine and the Hebrew Scripture. Michaelis wrote a review of Dohm's book, criticizing its recommendations and arguing that "it will be impossible to consider the Jews as an equal of our citizens" (1782/2011: 35). Michaelis believed that Jews were especially deceitful, which he attributed to their national character. Although the Jewish character had praiseworthy elements, their national pride —reflected in their belief that they are the Chosen People— had corrupted them. Michaelis illustrated the alleged corruption by focusing on crimes committed by merchants and peddlers, particularly the offense of dealing in stolen goods. He contended that statistics show that Jews were overrepresented, relative to their share of the population, in the commission of those crimes.

Mendelssohn replied that, "where the wickedness of a people is to be evaluated one should not entirely overlook murderers, robbers, traitors, arsonists, adulterers, whores, killers of infants etc." (1783/2011: 40). Moreover, he pointed out that, even if one looked only at dealers in stolen goods, the appropriate baseline for judgment was not the Jewish share of the overall population but their share of merchants, among whom Jews were disproportionally represented due to longstanding legal restrictions on the sorts of jobs they could hold. Additionally, Mendelssohn noted that the economic opportunities Christians enjoyed made their property crimes morally more problematic than the property crimes of Jews, whose opportunities were drastically restricted.

Mendelssohn believed that Jews could remain observant (i.e., obeying the halakhah) while becoming equal citizens of the states in which they resided. A prominent representative of Enlightenment thinking, he saw no conflict between the requirements of Jewish law and the study of science, philosophy, and literature, and, to that extent, he rejected the assumption that customary Jewish practices necessarily reflected those requirements. In Mendelssohn's view, observant Jews could become fully integrated into European society, despite what Jewish traditionalists and Christian opponents of Jewish emancipation claimed. But he would die before any country in Europe took the step of making Jews equal citizens.

III. Progress and Pushback

Equal legal rights for Jews were first realized, not in the Prussia of Mendelssohn and Dohm or in the

Habsburg lands of Joseph II, but in France in the wake of its revolution against the *ancien régime*. The first step was the extension of full citizenship to the Sephardic Jews living in the south of France and on the Atlantic coast, who were more assimilated into European culture —its forms of dress and personal appearance and its secular life— than the Ashkenazi Jews of eastern France. A year later the Ashkenazis gained citizenship. The result was that by 1792 Jewish men could qualify for active citizenship, even as all women —whether Christian or Jewish— were relegated to second-class citizenship by the Constitution of 1791, a document reflecting Sieyès' views on the matter (see Chapter Two, sec. II).

The achievement of equal civil rights for Jews was accompanied by a rejection of the communal autonomy that Jews had traditionally enjoyed. Civil rights belonged to individuals, not to communities. Clermont-Tonnere, a deputy in the National Assembly and advocate of equality for Jews, put his position on the matter in a dramatic way during the debates in the assembly: "The Jews should be denied everything as a nation, but granted everything as individuals" (Flohr-Mendes and Reinharz 2011: 124). And the official decree of emancipation reflected his view, guaranteeing equal rights to Jews who took the oath of citizenship and providing that the taking of the oath by Jews "shall be considered as a renunciation of all privileges in their favor" (Law Relating to the Jews 1791).

Equal citizenship for Jews did not last long in France, as Napoleon's decree of 1808 abridged their civil rights, placing special restrictions on their economic activities and limiting their rights of residency. The decree was to be in force for ten years, "in the hope that, at the end of this period and as a result of these various measures made necessary because of the Jews, there will no longer be any difference between them and the other citizens of our Empire" (Napoleon 1808/2011: 162). Napoleon had explicitly repudiated the decision of the revolutionary government to make Jews equal citizens, instead following the view of Joseph II that Jews needed to prove their moral regeneration before equality could be granted. And although Napoleon's European conquests did bring some degree of emancipation, there was considerable pushback from the local Christian populations, who succeeded for a time in derailing the extension of legal rights to Jews.

The pushback was not limited to uneducated Christian peasants. In 1831, Heinrich Paulus, a distinguished professor of theology wrote, "As long as Jews believe that their continued existence as Jews must be in accordance with the Rabbinic-Mosaic spirit, no nation could grant them civil rights ... because they apparently wish to remain a nation apart" (Mendes-Flohr and Reinharz 2011: 166). By persisting in their adherence to Jewish law and taking themselves to be part of a nation scattered across the world in the Diaspora, Jews had no claim to be equal citizens of the nations in which they lived. Moreover, Paulus was calling into question the political loyalty of Jews; he was suggesting that they were loyal to worldwide Jewry, not to the particular state on whose territory they resided. And Paulus's skepticism about Jewish political loyalty would be conveyed over the decades by the often-used pejorative description of Jews as a "nation within a nation."

Jewish emancipation was facilitated by the emergence of forms of Judaism that revised, reinterpreted, or rejected various elements of the traditional form. One element that bore on the issue of Jewish loyalty to the state concerned the traditional prayers asking for the Messiah to come and bring an end to the Diaspora by gathering the world's Jews together in their ancestral land. In the eyes of many Christians, it seemed contradictory to offer such prayers and also to profess loyalty to the particular nation in which one resided. Jews who favored emancipation needed to address the claim that there was such a contradiction.

In 1845, a conference of leaders of Reform Judaism adopted a resolution that "[t]he messianic idea should receive prominent mention in ... prayer, but all petitions for our return to the land of our fathers and for the restoration of a Jewish state should be eliminated from the liturgy" (Mendes-Flohr and Reinharz 2011: 208).

The resolution rested on a radical reinterpretation of the idea of the Messiah, construing it as a religious but not political concept. The very distinction between the religious and the political was foreign to the traditional understanding of the idea, but the distinction was very much in keeping with the modern secular state.

By the end of the 19th century, Jews were equal citizens under the law in most European states, with the main exceptions of czarist Russia, where five million Jews resided, and Romania. In the wake of the assassination of the reformist Czar Alexander II in 1881, the limited rights that had been granted to Russian Jews were rescinded, and a wave of pogroms swept across the country. Romania had legal restrictions on Jewish residency, property ownership and access to the professions, and placed legal obstacles in the path of Jews seeking to obtain citizenship.

Yet, even in those European countries where Jews had gained the same civil rights as Christians, they often found that popular anti-Semitism limited their opportunities. In Germany, for example, anti-Semitism led to the *de facto* exclusion of Jews from positions in government and from membership in student fraternities and the other associations of civil society, notwithstanding the legal equality of Jews. They were not formally excluded from official positions but were deemed unsuitable for them by the authorities who administered the state bureaucracy. And the associations of German civil society, exercising their collective rights as voluntary organizations and driven by anti-Semitism, systematically chose to close their membership to Jews. The prominent German historian Heinrich von Treitschke expressed the attitude of many of his compatriots in the final decades of the 19th century when he wrote that "the Jews are our misfortune" (1879).

Thus, the granting of formal legal rights meant that Jews were equal under the law, but it did not mean that they were equal members of society. The problem was not that the laws were deliberately flouted, but rather that the background beliefs and attitudes of European society meant that the laws were applied in discriminatory ways and valuable social opportunities were routinely denied. One general lesson illustrated by Jewish emancipation, the American Civil Rights Movement and, as we will see in the next chapter, the women's movements of the 19th and 20th centuries, is that genuine equality of citizenship for the members of previously subordinated and stigmatized groups depends on much more than legal reforms. Substantial changes in the way those groups are typically perceived within society are indispensable as well.

It would be a mistake to think, though, that formal legal rights meant nothing to 19th century European Jews. Their legal rights made it possible for Jews to pursue educational, economic and political opportunities that they had previously lacked. More generally, gaining formal legal rights contributed to the improvement of the life-prospects of European Jews, even if anti-Semitism meant that such rights were not sufficient to bring equal citizenship. But their situation did not appear promising to many Jews, especially those of the working-class, at the end of the 19th and in the early 20th centuries. They embraced political Zionism, a nationalist movement founded by Theodor Herzl and aiming to build a Jewish state somewhere outside of Europe.

Herzl held that anti-Semitism doomed the effort of European Jews to achieve equal citizenship. He wrote, "No one can deny the gravity of the situation of the Jews. Wherever they live in perceptible numbers, they are more or less persecuted. Their equality before the law, granted by statute, has become practically a dead letter" (1896/1988: 85). And on Herzl's account, European Jews suffered the worst of both worlds: emancipation not only failed to produce genuine equality, but it also provoked hostility toward Jews. The reason was that emancipation brought some Jews into the middle-class, where Christians saw them as unwelcome competitors. Accordingly, Herzl claimed that the persecution of Jews would continue "in every country ... even in those most highly civilized ... until the Jewish question finds a solution on a political basis" (76). The proffered political solution was the establishment of a sovereign state in which Jews would collectively govern themselves.

Looking back from the perspective of the world after the Holocaust, Herzl is sometimes seen as a prophet who foresaw that a Jewish state was needed to avert Jewish catastrophe. But his understanding of even his own era was flawed. Jews existed in "perceptible numbers" in America, but, while they were subjected to social discrimination and the large influx of them escaping pogroms and economic destitution in eastern Europe exacerbated anti-Semitism, American Jews were not persecuted. Moreover, it was self-contradictory for Herzl to claim that emancipation in Europe was "practically a dead letter," while also holding that emancipation brought Jews into the middle-class. There were many paths that history could have taken in the first four decades of the 20th century. It is highly likely that none of them would have seen the elimination of anti-Semitism, but a number would have involved a more progressive realization of equal citizenship for Jews, with or without a Jewish state.

Chapter 6
Women and Equality

I. Three Waves?

According to the conventional account of feminism, there have been three feminist waves in modern history. The first developed in the mid-19th century and extended until 1920. Its main success is said to have been the achievement of the franchise for women in many Western countries. The second wave developed in the mid-1960's and lasted until the mid-1980's. Its main success is said to have been legislation prohibiting sex discrimination in employment, education and other major arenas of modern life. The third developed in the mid-1990's and continues to this day. Its main achievement is said to be, not so much political or legal as intellectual, namely, making feminist thought more responsive than it had previously been to the distinctive concerns of women who were not White, middle-class, or heterosexual.

As with the conventional periodization of the Civil Rights Movement, this account of feminism has been challenged by many scholars. The historian Dorothy Cobble writes that, instead of thinking about discrete waves, we should proceed from the premise that "there are always movements for freedom and equality among women in every era, among every generation" (Laughlin 2010: 90). In a similar vein, other historians object to the wave metaphor on the ground that it elides feminist activism and theorizing in the periods between the putative waves. And it can be said that the same elision occurs with respect to feminist activity prior to the onset of the first wave.

The intellectual seeds for the women's movements that developed across many countries in the 19th century had been planted in the closing decade of the 18th, when Enlightenment ideas led a few persons to argue for the civil and political equality of women. In England, perhaps the most prominent, pre-wave feminist voice was that of Mary Wollstonecraft, who criticized the exclusion of women from the full scope of natural rights recognized as belonging to men. She wrote that even the men of the Enlightenment who brought the revolution to France have kept women in subjection "by denying them civil and political rights, to remain immured in their families groping in the dark" (1792/1988: 5). She insisted that women were as capable as men of developing and exercising the powers of reason, and it was such a capability that grounded the claim to rights for men and women alike. At the same time, Wollstonecraft thought that the traditional upbringing of women had left them unprepared to develop their rational capacities and fulfill their responsibilities to society. Only radical changes in the socialization and education of women would enable them to live by the dictates of reason and throw off the yoke of their subjugation to men.

On Wollstonecraft's account, there was a striking analogy between the social status of men *qua* men and that of the hereditary aristocracy. Men and aristocrats alike enjoyed a raft of inherited privileges and prerogatives that they had done nothing to earn and that reflected no merit or excellence on their part. And the system of "male aristocracy," she wrote, meant that "[t]he rights of humanity have been ... confined to the male line from Adam downwards" (87). Moreover, women lived "[c]onfined in cages, like the feathered race [and] have nothing to do but plume themselves" (56). They were expected to beautify themselves so as to be pleasing to men but also to be dependent on men and obedient to them. And socialization operated on women and men to ensure that most came to internalize these expectations.

Equality for women required, as Wollstonecraft saw matters, dramatic changes in the attitudes, actions and expectations of men but also of women. She wrote, "It is time to effect a revolution in female manners, time to restore to them their lost dignity, and ... make them ... labour by reforming themselves to reform the world" (45). Wollstonecraft regarded the needed changes as a kind of moral regeneration that would bring about a much more complete realization of women's capacities for rationality and virtue. However, like Dohm in his analysis of Jewish emancipation, she did not regard those changes as a precondition for equal citizenship but rather as a consequence of it. She argued that, because the distinctive deficiencies of women were the product of their gender-specific upbringing and their assigned place in society, "it is reasonable to suppose that they will change their character, and correct their vices and follies, when they are allowed to be free in a physical, moral, and civil sense" (194).

II. Aims of the Early Women's Movements

One of the key elements of the patriarchal ideology that kept women in a subordinate position was the notion that their childbearing capacity defined their nature and destined them to a highly restrictive set of social roles and opportunities. In the 1872 case of Bradwell v. Illinois, the U.S. Supreme Court gave clear expression to that ideology. The court upheld a decision of the state's highest court that rejected the application of Myra Bradwell, on grounds of her sex, to practice law in Illinois. In its opinion, the Supreme Court wrote, "The paramount destiny and mission of woman are to fulfill the noble and benign offices of wife and mother. This is the law of the Creator" (141). Women were, by nature, unfit for the practice of law and for much else besides; the only suitable roles for them were connected to bearing and raising children and caring for their husband and household.

As part of the effort to combat this patriarchal ideology, access to education became one of the first aims of the feminist movements that emerged during the 19th century. Such access was understood as crucial for women who sought to improve their economic and social situation. High school level education for girls was nonexistent or dealt mainly with matters of home-making, and, in many European states, women were denied the opportunity to study at universities. France first allowed women to attend lectures at the Sorbonne in 1880, and women were permitted full-time study at German universities only in the first decade of the 20th century.

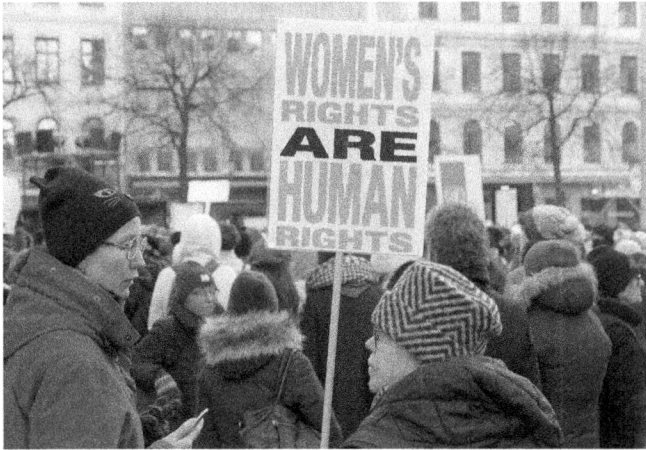

3. Women's March, a global protest for women's rights in central Stockholm, Sweden, January 21, 2018.

Another aim of feminism in the 19th century was the repeal of the laws that treated women as essentially minors, unable to enter contracts, own property, and receive income, among many other legal disabilities. Under the English common-law doctrine of coverture, a wife had no independent legal personality from that of her husband. In his classic compendium of English law, Blackstone formulated the doctrine in the following way: "By marriage, the husband and wife are one person in law: that is, the very being or legal existence of the woman is suspended during the marriage, or at least is incorporated and consolidated into that of the husband" (1803/1996: 441). France had its own version of coverture, treating adult women as legal minors under the supervision of their fathers or husbands.

During the late 19th century, securing the franchise became the central goal of women's movements around the world. In 1894, New Zealand was the first country to enact female suffrage, but most nations did not follow suit until after World War I. Until the first decade of the 20th century, women in much of Germany and in Austria were even legally barred from joining political groups or parties.

Gaining the right to vote was the signal achievement of the "first wave" of feminism, but one should also acknowledge the significance of other substantial strides that were taken toward equality under the law, including the dismantling of the doctrine of coverture. In the U.S., coverture was eliminated over the course of the 19th century on a state-by-state basis, and, in Britain, statutes granting property rights to married women gradually undermined the doctrine. However, France did not make married women legally independent persons until 1938.

As for the franchise, women's voting did not change the political landscape, despite the hope of many that the politics of women would be more humane than that of men. Women's votes did not keep nations from plunging into two devastating world wars. Additionally, after both wars, societies in Europe and North America took a conservative turn that affirmed with renewed vigor the notion that the so-called "destiny and mission of woman" were to be a wife and mother. Further feminist activity would be needed to directly challenge that notion and seriously weaken its hold on society.

The idea that women are not fit for equality and do not want it has been a persistent theme of the patriarchal ideology that has undergirded the male domination of society. Even after World War II, in which millions of women in Allied nations contributed to the war effort by taking jobs in defense industries and working in the underground resistance to the Nazis, the idea remained very much alive. Women were held to be irrational and emotional and to want the strong and steady hand of a man with authority over them. In a more nuanced version of the argument, the possibility was conceded that women were as capable as men of being rational and self-controlled and that unequal conditions might well have made women irrational and emotional; but it was then asserted that, because they were still irrational and emotional, women were not yet fit for equality. Sieyès' rejection of active citizenship for women in the wake of the French Revolution suggests just such an argument (see Chapter Two, sec. II).

The 20th century French philosopher Simone de Beauvoir understood that arguments like that of Sieyès would condemn women to perpetual inequality through a vicious circle in which women would be entitled to equality only if their inequality had already been eliminated. She also realized that the same kind of argument had been used repeatedly in history by conservatives resisting the extension of equality to excluded groups (see Chapter Four, sec. VI). Thus, she wrote, "Without a doubt, if a caste is maintained in an inferior position, it remains inferior: but freedom can break the circle; let blacks vote and they become worthy of the vote; give woman responsibilities and she knows how to assume them" (1949/2010: 860). In Beauvoir's view, the solution to the vicious circle that threatened the extension of equality came from the combination of political action and the human freedom possessed by men and women, Whites and Blacks.

III. The 1960's, 70's and Beyond

Among the main targets of the feminists who rose to prominence in the "second wave" was what John Stuart Mill had called "social tyranny" (1859/2010: 7). Some forms of tyranny, he explained, operated through laws and other official acts. But another, less noticed form operated through informal social norms, which embodied the prevailing expectations of the majority and enforced those expectations, not through legal punishment, but rather through social condemnation, criticism and ostracism. The penalties were usually not as severe as the punishments imposed by tyranny operating through the law, but social tyranny "leaves fewer means of escape, penetrating much more deeply into the details of life, and enslaving the soul itself" (7). His point was that the desires and aspirations of individuals will typically form in a way that reflects social expectations.

For Mill, the subjugation of women was the most striking case of social tyranny. He described how it operated:

> All women are brought up from the very earliest years in the belief that their ideal of character is the very opposite to that of men; not self-will, and government by self-control, but submission, and yielding to the control of others. All the moralities tell them that it is the duty of women and ... their nature to live for others; to make complete abnegation of themselves, and to have no life but in their affections (1869/2010: 265).

Mill recognized that the forces of women's socialization that he described were not completely effective in all women, but the forces were very effective in many, "enslaving the soul itself."

In line with Mill's account, feminists of the 1960's and 70's advocated "consciousness raising," a process through which women could, through discussion with other women, presumably liberate themselves from the social forces that enslaved their souls and limited their lives. Democratic societies did not legally prohibit women from practicing law or medicine, entering business, conducting scientific research, becoming university faculty, or pursuing any of the other prestigious and lucrative professions that men monopolized. But social expectations continued to forcefully steer women's desires and thoughts in the traditional direction. Feminists sought to disrupt those expectations and a host of social norms that arbitrarily constricted the opportunities of women.

The feminist movement of the second wave was not monolithic. Roughly speaking, it could be divided into a more radical wing and a more liberal one. The differences were over how men should be viewed, whether law and litigation were valuable tools for fighting patriarchy, and what role capitalism played in the perpetuation of patriarchy.

Radicals saw society as a system of male supremacy, akin to the oppressive systems of White supremacy in the Jim Crow South and apartheid South Africa. In their manifesto, the radical group Redstockings declared, "All men receive economic, sexual, and psychological benefits from male supremacy. All men have oppressed women" (Redstockings 1969). As a result of their experience in anti-capitalist/anti-Vietnam war groups, such as the Students for a Democratic Society, where men dominated discussion and decision making and marginalized women members, radical feminists concluded that women-only groups were essential elements in their liberation. Their consciousness-raising groups were a key part of this approach.

Radical feminists were also skeptical about whether law and litigation could do much to eliminate women's oppression. Carol Hanisch, a prominent radical who coined the phrase 'the personal is political' (1969), criticized leading liberal feminists such as Betty Friedan and Gloria Steinem because they "refuse to name men as the enemy" and "talk about women's oppression as a legal question, as if getting some legislation passed would solve our situation." The liberals thereby failed to pose a serious threat to male power and domination. For Hanisch and the other radicals, 'the personal is political' did not mean that there was a legislative fix to the oppression that women suffered in their personal lives or beyond; it meant that patriarchy did not stop at the threshold of the home or the bedroom and that women were thereby called upon to challenge male supremacy in all spheres of their lives, including the putatively "private" sphere of personal relations.

Liberals saw society as plagued by widespread discrimination against women but generally avoided the charge that all men oppressed women and were the enemy. Liberals held that, even though many women were unhappy in their intimate heterosexual relationships, men were not an enemy but, potentially, an ally, because they too were harmed by sex discrimination. And liberals were more open than radicals to working together in the same groups with men to combat sex discrimination and saw more value in law and litigation for eliminating such discrimination. The Civil Rights Act of 1964 had prohibited discrimination based on sex, and liberals believed that the act could be used, along with new legislative initiatives, to advance women's equality.

Radicals and liberals also disagreed over the role that capitalism played in the oppression of women. While liberals called for extensive social programs to help women, radicals called for a revolution against capitalism to go hand-in-hand with the destruction of patriarchy and racism as well. Liberals were not libertarian advocates of minimal government but rather proponents of an activist state that would, for example, provide universal, publicly-funded childcare. But radicals thought that such liberal programs failed to recognize that male supremacy, White supremacy, and capitalist arrangements formed a single system of oppression that needed to be totally destroyed. Accordingly, Kathie Sarachild, a founder of Redstockings, criticized liberals for wanting "to get women back to tending their normal business of putting patches on the wounds of the same old rotten system of male supremacy, racism and capitalism" (1978: 23).

The liberal-radical division is, admittedly, a conceptual simplification. There are coherent ways in which different aspects of each view can be combined. It is possible, for example, to conjoin the liberal position that legislation and litigation can make significant progress toward equality with the radical idea that all men benefit from the oppression of women. Still, many real-world political and theoretical disputes between women fell along liberal-radical lines. Hanisch was giving voice to the radical side of those disputes when she condemned what she saw as "[t]he liberal takeover of women's liberation" (1978: 163).

In certain respects, liberal feminism was like the mainstream civil rights view and radical feminism like the Black Power perspective. How valuable are litigation and legislation in correcting the injustices imposed on women/Blacks? To what degree will men/Whites be helpful, or obstructive, in promoting the goals of women's/Black freedom and equality? Is some revolutionary socialist alternative to capitalism needed for women/Blacks to achieve their rightful freedom and equality? Liberal feminists and mainstream civil rights activists tended to line up on one side of those questions, while radical feminists and Black Power activists generally lined up on the other.

As with Jewish emancipation and the freedom struggles of American Blacks, an important lesson of the history of the movements for women's rights was that formal equality under the law was insufficient for genuinely equal citizenship. Even when the laws were not directly subverted or flouted, as happened regularly with Jim Crow, background social norms turned formal equality into actual inequality. It mattered that, under the law, women had the right to pursue any career that they chose, but it also mattered that informal norms powerfully discouraged women from imagining themselves as pursuing any path in life other than "the noble and benign offices of wife and mother" (Bradwell v. Illinois: 141).

Nonetheless, working in combination with changing social attitudes supportive of women's rights, laws prohibiting sex discrimination seem to have had a substantial effect in promoting equality. In the U.S. the law known as "Title IX" (1972) banned any education program that received federal funding from discriminating against persons on the basis of sex. The law applied to athletic as well as academic programs. From 1972 forward, the proportion of females participating in high school and college sports increased dramatically, so that, by 2016, the rate of participation had risen ten times for high school girls and seven times for college women (National Coalition 2017: 38). The percentage of women among professors in science and engineering rose from under 5% in 1972 to more than 20% by 2013 (18, Figure 5). One might contend that these and similar increases were due solely to changing attitudes, not to Title IX. But such a contention is dubious, at least when it comes to women's participation in sports, where enforcement of Title IX by the federal government was vigorous. The government formulated rules specifying what participation rates schools needed to have in order to comply with the law, and compliance was closely monitored by the schools themselves and the government. Schools did not want to lose federal funding by being found noncompliant.

Additionally, we should keep in mind the interplay of law and social attitudes. The law reflects social attitudes, but it also serves as an authoritative symbolic affirmation of certain of those attitudes and a rejection of others. Such affirmations and rejections are bound to influence some part of the population, and Title IX stood for the rejection of sexist stereotypes that hindered women's access to sports and education.

It was not uncommon in 1972 for people to think that females were inherently much less interested in sports than men were and much less suited than men to participate in them. The view was an aspect of the attitude, expressed in the Bradwell case, that the proper and natural social role of women was to serve as wife and mother. Strenuous athletic training and competition were seen as jeopardizing a woman's childbearing capacity and as incompatible with the role of motherhood. It was this kind of attitude that led Boston Marathon officials in 1966 to reject Roberta Gibbs's attempt to register for the race and the next year prompted one official to physically assault Katherine Switzer, who had registered as K.V. Switzer and was able to start the race, in an effort to stop her from running (both women managed to complete the marathon).

It was also not uncommon in 1972 for people to think that the proper and natural female role in society meant that access to higher education was less valuable to them than it was to men. In another aspect of the Bradwell mentality, the thinking was that women went to college to find husbands, who would pursue careers as the women raised their children, and not to prepare for a career of their own.

Title IX was a decisive repudiation of the Bradwell mentality by the highest political institutions in the country. They were sending a clear message: when it comes to education, sexist attitudes were insupportable. Even before Title IX, the women's movement had succeeded in moving a significant segment of the population away from such attitudes, making it possible for Congress and the President to support the law. But it is also reasonable to hold that Title IX, in turn, helped to move some of the population away from sexist attitudes by signaling that traditional stereotypes that impeded the access of females to educational programs and activities were to be rejected.

Nonetheless, in the U.S., the most striking repudiation of sexist attitudes would have been the Equal Rights Amendment (ERA). The amendment provided, "Equality of rights under the law shall not be denied or abridged by the United States or by any state on account of sex," and empowered Congress to enforce such equality by "appropriate legislation." Congress passed the amendment in 1972, six decades after an initial version had been introduced, but the amendment was vigorously opposed by conservative forces claiming that it would harm women by subjecting them to the military draft, taking away their alimony, requiring unisex restrooms, and otherwise depriving them of special protections that they enjoyed.

After the amendment failed to receive the ratification of the requisite number of states before the 1982 deadline set by Congress had expired, it was generally regarded as legally dead. In recent years, however, a few additional states have ratified the ERA, pushing the total number of ratifications over the threshold and leading some to hope that the amendment could still become part of the Constitution. But the additional ratifications were more than thirty years after the congressional deadline, and several states had rescinded their ratifications prior to that deadline. Perhaps Congress can waive the deadline and states cannot validly rescind ratification, but it is difficult to think that America's courts would rule in that way without a major shift in judicial ideology.

It is reasonable to think that the ERA would have significantly advanced the equal citizenship of women. Had the amendment become law, a strong message would have been sent to the country that women are to be equal citizens. But the history of the Civil War Amendments and the Supreme Court's interpretation of them shows that even clear legal affirmations of equality can be undermined by hostile judicial interpretations. As we have seen, the Supreme Court gave constricted interpretations of the meaning of those amendments, often defeating their letter and spirit (Chapter Four, section III). It is entirely possible that much of the progressive potential of the ERA would have been undercut by the court's interpretation.

Consider the case U.S. v. Morrison (2000), which involved the federal Violence Against Women Act (VAWA 1994). Congress claimed the power to enact the law under the Commerce Clause and the 14th Amendment, and one provision of VAWA allowed female victims of violence to sue their attacker in federal court for gender-motivated violence. In the Morrison case, the Supreme Court ruled that the provision was unconstitutional because it exceeded the lawful powers of Congress. The court held that the Commerce Clause applied only to conduct that was essentially economic in nature and that the category 'gender-motivated violence' failed to meet that requirement. And citing the Civil Rights Cases (1883) as precedent, the court affirmed its longstanding doctrine that the 14th Amendment applied only to the actions of states, not to the conduct of private individuals. Had the ERA been law, it would have provided a legal route for Congress to argue that the provision of VAWA in question was within its powers. But the court would likely have held the provision invalid anyway, arguing that the ERA applied only to government action, not to the conduct of private parties.

Chapter 7

Current Controversies

I. Same-Sex Marriage

Movements for women's equality confronted a social world in which males and females were inflexibly assigned roles from which individuals could deviate only at substantial risk of severe informal censure and, at times, formal legal punishment. Moreover, each individual was irreversibly assigned at birth to the category of male or female. As societies have moved in the direction of equality, allowing greater individual freedom than previously, gender roles have remained, nonetheless, a substantial social force. A distinction between male and female sexuality, appearance, and behavior is still very sharply drawn and strictly policed, and social norms demand that the individual's sex assignment at birth be their sexual identity for life. Gays, trans persons, and other gender nonconforming individuals run afoul of these social demands concerning sexuality and sexual identity.

In some countries, the civil rights of gays have been increasingly recognized over the past two decades. Same-sex marriage, for example, now exists in well over a dozen nations. However, there is much of the world in which grave legal and social risks attend to being openly gay and same-sex marriage is out of the question.

4. Students protesting with banners on June 25, 2010 in Toronto, Canada.

The right to get married is a civil right, on any reasonable account, and so arbitrary restrictions on the right are civil rights violations. Historically, the most prominent example of an arbitrary restriction is to be found in laws that did not permit racial intermarriage. The U.S. once had the world's harshest anti-miscegenation laws, with 30 states not only invalidating interracial marriages but providing for criminal penalties for the persons who sought to enter such marriages. Many countries have had laws disallowing interracial marriages, but the U.S. was alone in criminally punishing them. That is, it was alone until the Nazis adopted their infamous "Blood Law" (1935), which criminalized marriage between Jews and persons of "German blood" (Whitman 2017). Nazi ideology regarded Jews as constituting a race, and Nazi jurists explicitly looked to American race law when they developed their Blood Law.

It was not until 1967 that the U.S. Supreme Court declared unconstitutional laws prohibiting racial intermarriage (Loving v. Virginia). At the time, sixteen states in the Union had such laws. The Lovings were an interracial couple who had been charged with violating Virginia's ban on miscegenation. They pled guilty, and the trial judge gave them a one-year sentence, suspended on the condition that they leave the state and not return for 25 years. The judge wrote, "Almighty God created the races white, black, yellow, malay and red, and he placed them on separate continents ... The fact that he separated the races shows that he did not intend for the races to mix" (3).

The Lovings later sought to have the judgment of the trial court vacated, and the case ended up before the Supreme Court. In its argument, Virginia defended its anti-miscegenation statute on the ground that it did not amount to invidious discrimination, because it provided for the same punishment for Blacks and Whites. However, the court saw the statute as a measure intended to support White supremacy and, accordingly, struck it down as a violation of the 14th Amendment's guarantee of equal protection.

Proponents of same-sex marriage perceive a parallel between anti-miscegenation laws and laws disallowing marriage between partners of the same sex. They argue that it is arbitrary to restrict marriage to heterosexual couples, even if only heterosexual couples can produce children. Sterile heterosexual couples have a right to marry, despite the fact that they cannot reproduce, and so same-sex couples cannot be reasonably denied the right on the ground that they are unable to reproduce. Moreover, same-sex couples can raise (adopted) children and share the benefits and burdens of life just as heterosexual couples do. As the philosopher Stephen Macedo writes, "all of the goods that can be shared by sterile heterosexual couples can also be shared by committed homosexual couples" (1996: 39).

Girgis, Anderson, and George argue that the defense of same-sex marriage rests on a faulty understanding of marriage, deriving from the sexual revolution of the 1960's and repudiating the view that had prevailed in almost every society until then. On the older, traditional view, which Girgis and his coauthors defend, marriage is a permanent commitment, "ordered to procreation and family life" and constituting a "comprehensive union" of a man and a woman (2012: 7). The union joins spouses "in body as well as in mind" and is "sealed by sexual intercourse" (3). Such a union is "a basic human good, a distinctive way of thriving" (35). And "there is something special" about a marital couple's sexual intercourse, because it constitutes the "highest kind of bodily unity" (26), a unity not available in any other kind of relationship. By contrast, the more recent and, as Girgis and his coauthors hold, mistaken view of marriage regards it as essentially a matter of living together and having a strong emotional connection. On that view, when the emotions cool, the partners might reasonably seek to end their marriage.

However, *contra* Girgis and his coauthors, the defense of same-sex marriage need not regard marriage as simply a matter of emotional union and cohabitation. Instead, the defense can argue that there are substantial goods to marriage that do not depend on heterosexual intercourse and that go beyond being emotionally connected and living together. Security in a stable relationship that is publicly and legally ratified as lasting and exclusive is among those goods.

Girgis thinks that the traditional understanding of marriage reflects its true nature, but the understanding appears to have been repudiated by most democratic societies since the liberalization of marriage laws and norms that began with the 19th century rejection of the law of coverture. As we have seen in our discussion of women's equality (Chapter Six, section II), over the course of a century, coverture was limited and eventually eliminated in favor of legal equality between husband and wife, though traditionalists repeatedly argued that such changes violated the essence of marriage as a union in which "the very being or legal existence of the woman is suspended … or at least is incorporated and consolidated into that of the husband" (Blackstone 1803/1996: 441).

Changes in the social understanding of marriage did not stop with the elimination of coverture. Subsequent transformations were reflected in the rejection of the requirement of sexual intercourse for the consummation of marriage, the spread of no-fault divorce laws, and the acceptance of pre-marital sex. Given that such radical changes in the understanding of marriage have taken place and been inscribed in law, it is unclear how law and society can now consistently or justly exclude same-sex couples from forming a marital bond. Moreover, despite the effort to distinguish laws against racial intermarriage from laws against same-sex-marriage, both types of law reflect a supremacist view: White supremacism, in the former case, and heterosexual supremacism in the latter.

The idea that there is something special about the sexual intercourse of a married couple is a piece of metaphysical speculation that, however widely-accepted in ages past, now provides scant justification for denying same-sex partners access to an important social good. From the perspective of the values and principles of contemporary democratic societies, restricting marriage on the basis of the idea is barely more persuasive than the defense of anti-miscegenation laws offered by the trial judge in the Loving case.

II. The Rights of Trans Persons

Discrimination against trans persons often has the same grounds as discrimination against gays. Consider the matter of employment discrimination. Gays and trans persons have been fired for their sexual orientation or gender presentation, and, in both sorts of cases, the employer has sought to uphold traditional views of male and female. And those traditional views are inextricably linked to social stereotypes and norms that arbitrarily constrain individual liberty. Males are supposed to appear and act in certain ways and females in another. But persons have a moral right to define their own sexuality and gender identity, and incursions on that right —like other rights— require strong justifying reasons in order to be acceptable. And there is no good reason for depriving persons of their livelihood because they choose to appear and act in ways that do not conform to the traditional expectations that attach to their presumed biological sex.

In its ruling in Bostock v. Georgia (2020), the U.S. Supreme Court found that, "[w]hen an employer fires an employee for being homosexual or transgender, it necessarily and intentionally discriminates against that individual in part because of sex. And that is all Title VII [of the 1964 Civil Rights Act] has ever demanded to establish liability" (14). The ruling has been celebrated by progressives, and its vindication of the rights of gay and trans employees is to be welcomed. However, it should be noted that the ruling rested on a rather controversial way of construing statutes and that it is unclear that, over a run of cases, such a method of statutory construction would be sufficiently protective of civil rights. The ruling was not based on any moral principle that might be seen as underlying the Civil Rights Act, such as a principle condemning gender stereotypes that arbitrarily constrain individual liberty, but rather on the meaning of the word 'sex'. The employees won because, had they been a different sex, then, all else held constant, their employers would not have fired them. For example, a woman employee would not have been fired for having sexual relations with a man, but a male employee was fired for the same conduct. Such is discrimination based on "sex."

But consider the legal case of Johnson v. Santa Clara County Transportation Agency (1987). The case involved a legal challenge to the county's voluntary affirmative action plan, which gave a preference to women who were applying for promotion to jobs at the agency that had been traditionally reserved for men. Those jobs generally carried greater authority and remuneration than the jobs available to women. But a man who had applied for a promotion to one of the favored jobs was denied the position in favor of a woman, and he sued the agency, claiming that his rights under the Civil Rights Act of 1964 had been violated. The trial court agreed with him, arguing that giving preference to the woman because she was a woman amounted to illegal employment discrimination based on sex. However, the Supreme Court disagreed, holding that the agency's plan was consistent with the Civil Rights Act, because the plan "represent[ed] a moderate, flexible, case-by-case approach to effecting a gradual improvement in the representation of minorities and women in the Agency's workforce" (642). Accordingly, the court interpreted the act as compatible with measured efforts by employers to reduce the effects of traditional gender stereotypes.

By contrast with that interpretation, the reasoning in Bostock v. Georgia leads to the same conclusion that the trial court in the Santa Clara County case arrived at, namely, that the language of the Civil Rights Act is an absolute bar to any voluntary plan that aims to increase the representation of women in jobs traditionally reserved for men. It is hardly clear that women's equality would have been well-served by such a conclusion had the Supreme Court seen fit to accept it at the time, and, despite the celebration of the ruling in Bostock by progressives, its reading of the Civil Rights Act might lead to decisions in cases concerning gender and race that progressives deplore.

III. The "Burqa Bans"

During the early decades of the 21st century, a heated public debate developed in Europe concerning the Muslim inhabitants of the continent. The debate was intensified when a large influx of mostly Muslim refugees from war zones in the Middle East entered the region. Many Europeans objected to the influx, not only on the ground of its size, but also because they held that the refugees, due to their religious beliefs and practices, were unlikely to become good citizens. Muslims were said to embrace values antagonistic to European ones and to be largely unassimilable into European societies. To forestall the feared "Islamization," a number of countries enacted laws that restricted Muslim practices. The most widely discussed of those laws have been the so-called "burqa bans," which prohibit the wearing of facial coverings in public places. More than a dozen European states have enacted such bans, including France, Switzerland, Denmark, Austria, and Belgium. In addition, even before the influx of Muslim refugees, Switzerland had adopted by referendum a ban on the construction of minarets. Like the burqa bans, the Swiss referendum was motivated by the perception that the culture of the country was being taken over by alien values.

5. Protest in George Square against racism, Glasgow (Scotland). August, 31, 2019.

Despite the protests of human rights organizations that burqa bans violated Europe's Convention on Human Rights, in S.A.S. v. France (2014), the European Court of Human Rights (ECHR) upheld France's ban on wearing a facial covering in public. The court ruled that the French law did not violate the human rights to privacy and religious freedom of Muslim women. France had acted within its "margin of appreciation," a zone of discretion in which each country has the authority to interpret human rights requirements in terms of its own national values. The ECHR held that the ban was justified insofar as it sought "to secure the conditions whereby individuals can live together in their diversity" (para. 141). The ability of individuals who interacted in public spaces to see each other's uncovered face was reasonably regarded, in the court's view, as a condition needed for the members of a diverse population to live together.

The court's reasoning is unconvincing. Living together in diversity was what the Muslim woman challenging the ban was aiming to achieve. The ban hardly promoted diversity in its treatment of Muslim women who regard the wearing of facial coverings as an expression of their Islamic values. As Martha Nussbaum notes, "What inspires fear and mistrust in Europe, clearly, is not [facial] covering per se, but Muslim covering" (2010). Europeans did not think that ski masks impeded "living together." Instead, they raised their objections only against facial coverings that represented a person's commitment to Islam.

The anti-Muslim prejudice that is widespread in Europe echoes in certain respects European anti-Semitism during the era of Jewish emancipation. Like Muslims today, Jews were regarded as an alien element that could not be assimilated into Christian Europe. As we have seen (Chapter 5), at the same time that Christian Wilhelm von Dohm was proposing equal rights for Jews, the highly-respected Protestant biblical scholar, Johann Michaelis, argued that Jewish law made it impossible for Jews to become equal citizens. As long as Jews insisted on observing their dietary rules and refused to eat at Christian homes, "they will never become fully integrated in the way that Catholics, Lutherans, Germans, Wends, and French live together in one state" and so "it will be impossible to consider the Jew as an equal of our citizens and … therefore impossible to grant him the same freedoms" (Mendes-Flohr and Reinharz 2011: 35). Evidently, Michaelis was concerned that Jews and Christians could not "live together in their diversity"

Most advocates of the burqa bans will not explicitly declare that Muslims should not have the same freedoms as other citizens. But if the bans violate the right of Muslims to practice their religion, then the implication of the court's ruling in S.A.S is that Muslims do not have the same legal freedoms as others. Undoubtedly, the court would strike down laws that go much further than the burqa bans. It is difficult to think that it would let stand the extremist policies favored by the Dutch politician Geert Wilders, who has said, "Islam is something we can't afford any more in the Netherlands. I want the fascist Koran banned. We need to stop the Islamisation of the Netherlands. That means no more mosques, no more Islamic schools, no more imams" (Traynor 2008). Yet, by the extremity of their statements, Wilders and those of like mind have pushed the political discourse in a direction that makes it seem that the ruling in S.A.S. is a perfectly reasonable one.

Advocates of the burqa bans and other legal restrictions on Muslim practices often argue that Islam is hostile to individual rights that receive protection in liberal democracies in Europe and elsewhere, including the rights of gays, trans persons, and women. Accommodating Islam is said to endanger that protection.

In response, it should be pointed out that, even in liberal democracies, hostility toward gays and trans persons and male supremacist attitudes retain substantial strength among segments of the Christian and Jewish populations. Islam is far from the only religion with a record of such hostility and supremacism. Yet, no one argues that, for example, orthodox Jews should not be permitted to adopt their traditional mode of dress, because they are hostile to gay or trans rights and to equal rights for women. It might be said that most Jews have a more liberal mindset on issues of sex and gender than do the orthodox and that the proportion of Jews who embrace liberal values is greater than the proportion of Muslims who do so, but all that is beside the point. The individual Muslim, whether liberal or not, has just as much a right to wear her religious dress as does the individual Jew, whether liberal or not.

IV. Black Lives Matter

Black Lives Matter (BLM) is a movement that was founded in 2013 by the American activists Patrisse Khan-Cullors, Alicia Garza, and Opal Tometi. The movement fights against violence perpetrated by police and vigilantes against Blacks and members of other subordinated groups. Operating at the grassroots level and internationally as well, BLM affirms "the lives of Black queer and trans folks, disabled folks, undocumented folks, folks with records, women, and all Black lives along the gender spectrum." And alluding to the predominance of heterosexual men among the leaders of the mainstream and militant Black organizations that have fought for equality, like King's SCLC and the Black Panthers, the founders of BLM state, "Our network centers those who have been marginalized within Black liberation movements" (BLM: n.d.).

We have seen that violence against Blacks, perpetrated with impunity by White authorities and vigilantes, has been a central phenomenon in American history (Chapter Four). Even when the violence has been illegal according to the very rules laid down by the authorities, the Whites perpetrating it have repeatedly been immune from any legal repercussions. Few Whites would openly endorse Taney's declaration that Blacks "had no rights which the white man was bound to respect" (Finkelman: 2017: 61; see Chapter Four, section II), but the actions and attitudes of many Whites reveal a sharp discounting of the interests and agency of Blacks. White perpetrators of violence against Blacks continue to act with a sense of impunity, counting on other Whites to ensure that they escape punishment. And all-too-often the perpetrators continue to anticipate correctly the responses of other Whites.

Additionally, it is not simply the racially disproportionate number of police killings of Blacks that is at issue but the egregious nature of the killings as well: time and again, Blacks posing no threat to the officers or the public have been killed by police after being accused of petty offenses. These killings are flagrant violations of the civil rights of Blacks by persons who have a sworn duty to protect those rights. That same pattern of the flagrant abuse of power simply does not exist in the cases of Whites killed by police.

Moreover, police killings of Blacks are part of a larger picture in which White authorities and citizens act on the toxic presumption that Blacks are dangerous and up to no good. The presumption is manifested in the police practice of racial profiling, in which generalizations about the criminality of Blacks form the basis for efforts to detect and deter crime. And the presumption also finds expression in the widely documented phenomenon of Whites reporting to the police Blacks who are engaged in innocent activities but happen to be in places where Whites do not expect or want them to be.

6. Black lives matter protesters march in front of the City Hall following resolution on LAPD shooting death of African American woman Redel Jones. 12 July, 2016, Los Angeles.

The Black political scientist Adolf Reed has criticized BLM for diverting attention from "what might have been the focal point of critical discussion of police violence all along, that it is the product of an approach to policing that emerges from an imperative to contain and suppress the pockets of economically marginal and sub-employed working class populations produced by revanchist capitalism." Reed writes that "the evidence of gross racial disparity is clear: among victims of homicide by police blacks are represented at twice their rate of the population; whites are killed at somewhat less than theirs," but he adds that, "when we step away from focus on racial disproportions, the glaring fact is that whites are roughly half or nearly half of all those killed annually by police." Reed holds that, if we look beyond the anti-Black attitudes manifested in the killings, then we can see that "the deeper roots of the pattern of police violence [are] in enforcement of the neoliberal regime of sharply regressive upward redistribution and its social entailments" (2016).

However, it is unclear why we should "step away" from focusing on what Reed himself describes as a "gross racial disparity" in police killings. That disparity is not the only aspect of the killings that matter, but it is an aspect that should matter a great deal in a country like the U.S. in which the radical discounting of the lives of Blacks has had a long history and the presumption of Black criminality remains very much alive. The killing of economically-marginal, working class Whites by police should also matter a great deal in a country with a long history of licensing capital to set and coercively enforce the rules of economic and political life. But the slogan 'Black Lives Matter' should not be taken to mean that White lives do not matter or that Black lives matter more: it means that Black lives matter as well and as much.

Postscript

The history of civil rights movements is a story of progress and pushback. The pushback limited, and at times reversed, the progress. Sometimes the pushback has taken the form of naked violence, as in the bombings and beatings perpetrated by White supremacists in the South against American Blacks and their White allies during the classic period of the Civil Rights Movement. Sometimes the pushback has been more subtle, as in the resistance of German civil servants to admitting Jews to their number after Jews had gained equal legal rights. Sometimes the pushback has taken the form of political action aimed at blocking major progressive initiatives, as in the successful efforts of conservatives in the U.S. to prevent the Equal Rights Amendment from becoming law. And always the pushback takes the form of attitudes, practices, and institutions that were built around the assumption that the privileged properly have their elevated place in society. Those attitudes, practices, and institutions have an inertia that makes them difficult to alter, even though they are mutable human constructions. They form an entrenched framework of life that resists social movements seeking equal citizenship for the members of historically subordinated groups.

The efforts of the disabled to have their civil rights recognized and protected illustrate in a tangible way both the inertia and the mutability of the human constructions that block equal citizenship. Consider the U.S. Supreme Court case Tennessee v. Lane (2004), which concerned the power of Congress under the 14th Amendment to abrogate the immunity from private lawsuits that states have otherwise enjoyed under American constitutional doctrine. Tennessee was sued by two paraplegic persons who used wheelchairs and who asserted that the state provided no acceptable way for them to access courthouses that required individuals to mount stairs to gain entrance. One plaintiff was a defendant in a criminal trial, who literally had to crawl up the courthouse steps to appear for his case, and the other was a court reporter, who was unable to pursue her career. Their suit was brought under the Americans With Disabilities Act (ADA 1990), which prohibits public entities from denying any person their services or activities on account of disability. The construction of courthouses so that stairs provided the only mode of access had given no thought to any but the able-bodied. And even after Congress enacted the ADA, the Tennessee courthouses in question continued to stand unaltered, their stairs functioning as a physical obstacle preventing access to persons who were dependent on wheelchairs and who could have gained entry on their own accord if ramps had been installed. The lack of ramps combined with a stubborn indifference to the interests and agency of the physically handicapped to deprive them of their civil rights. In a 5-4 vote, the court upheld the power of Congress to make states liable to being sued for failing to eliminate such obstacles to equal citizenship.

In other instances, civil rights progress has been stymied by unyielding economic structures and policies that serve the interests of the privileged segments of society at the expense of the rest of the citizenry. We have seen that, during the American Civil Rights Movement, the mainstream leaders and their militant critics agreed that economic issues were of central importance (Chapter Four, section VII). Their common message, harkening back to the activists of the 1930's, was that substantive economic rights —rights to income, food, jobs and so on— were civil rights. The rationale behind the message was that secure access to the resources and opportunities needed to avoid economic hardship was required in order for the widely recognized civil rights —the rights to liberty and due process of law, for example, or, more recently, the rights to vote and hold public office— to have the practical value for persons that they were entitled to expect. The logic here was the same as that which led to the expansion of the idea of civil rights so that it came to encompass political rights.

However, unlike the case of political rights, the matter of whether or not substantive economic rights should be counted as civil rights remains highly contested, at least in America. In the post-war history of the U.S., except for a brief period in the 1960's, the idea that citizenship should carry claims to economic resources beyond what one could acquire through market arrangements was always treated as communistic and un-American by the dominant political, economic, and ideological powers. The result was that, in ensuing decades, the substantive economic demands of the classic civil rights era were forgotten by the country, even while it eventually came to lionize Martin Luther King and to celebrate the Civil Rights Movement.

In the rest of the world, the idea that rights to economic resources are civil rights has had a stronger foothold than in the U.S., due to the post-war strength of social democratic, labor, socialist, and communist parties. Even so, the ascendancy of neoliberal capitalism —a system in which capital flows without friction across borders while workers are trapped within their own countries, and markets are constructed according to the priorities of multinational corporations, hedge funds and banks— has pushed many nations to weaken the substantive economic rights of their citizens. Rich social democracies have been under increasing economic pressure to dial back their generous social insurance programs, and poor nations have been forced to bow to the demands of global capital. Nonetheless, resistance to those demands remains considerable, and the view has not yet been lost that civil rights include economic claims that go beyond whatever rights are recognized by existing market arrangements. The value of the idea of civil rights in the 21st century will depend in significant measure on whether or not it can be used to help states tame global capital and reconstruct markets so that the fundamental interests and human agency of citizens are respected and protected.

References

Legal Cases and Materials (U.S. Supreme Court opinions from 1991 to the present are available at *https://www.supremecourt.gov/opinions*; earlier opinions and American civil rights laws are available at *https://www.law.cornell.edu/*).

Americans with Disabilities Act (1990).

Bostock v. Clayton County, Georgia (2020) (slip opinion).

Bradwell v. Illinois 83 U.S. 130 (1872).

Civil Rights Act of 1870.

Civil Rights Act of 1875.

Civil Rights Act of 1964.

Civil Rights Act of 1968 (Fair Housing Act).

Civil Rights Cases 109 U.S. 3 (1883).

Cruikshank v. U.S. 92 U.S. 542 (1876).

Declaration of the Rights of Man and of the Citizen (France – 1789), available at *https://avalon.law.yale.edu/18th_century/rightsof.asp*.

Equal Rights Amendment (1972), available at *https://www.equalrightsamendment.org/*.

Executive Order 8802 (1941), available at *http://docs.fdrlibrary.marist.edu/od8802t.html*.

Fugitive Slave Act of 1793, available at *https://www.ushistory.org/presidentshouse/history/slaveact1793.php*.

Fugitive Slave Act of 1850, available at *https://avalon. law.yale.edu/19th_century/fugitive.asp*.

Heart of Atlanta Motel v U.S. 379 U.S. 241 (1964.)

International Covenant on Civil and Political Rights (1966), available at *https://www.ohchr.org/en/ professionalinterest/pages/ccpr.aspx*.

Johnson v. Santa Clara County Transportation Agency 480 U.S. 616 (1987).

Law Relating to the Jews (France 1791), available at *https:// www.marxists.org/history/france/revolution/1791/laws-jews.htm*.

Loving v. Virginia 388 U.S. 1 (1967).

Perez v. Brownell 356 US 44 (1958).

Plessy v. Ferguson 163 U.S. 537 (1896).

Prigg v. Pennsylvania 41 U.S. 539 (1842).

Roberts v. Boston 59 Mass. 198 (1849), available at *https:// cite.case.law/mass/59/198/?full_case=true&format=html*.

State v. Mann 13 N.C. 263 (1829).

Tennessee v. Lane 541 U.S. 509 (2004).

U.S. v. Morrison 529 U.S. 598 (2000).

U.S. v. Reese 92 U.S. 214 (1876).

Violence Against Women Act (1994).

Voting Rights Act of 1965.

Articles, Books, and other materials

Ahmann, Mathew et al. 1963. "March On Washington for Jobs and Freedom." Available at *https://www.crmvet.org/docs/mowprog.pdf*.

American Anthropological Association. 1947. "Statement on Human Rights," *American Anthropologist* 49: 539-543.

_____. 1999. "Declaration on Anthropology and Human Rights." Available at (*http://humanrights.americananthro.org/1999-statement-on-human-rights/1999*.

Arendt, Hannah. 1948/1994. *Origins of Totalitarianism*. New York: Harcourt.

Bauer, Bruno. 1843/1958. *The Jewish Problem*, Helen Lederer, trans. Cincinnati, Ohio: Hebrew Union College.

Beauvoir. Simone de. 1949/2010. *The Second Sex*. Constance Borde and Sheila Malovany-Chevallier, trans. New York: Vintage.

Bentham, Jeremy. 1843. "Anarchical Fallacies," in *The Works of Jeremy Bentham, vol. 2*. Available at *https://oll.libertyfund.org/titles/bentham-the-works-of-jeremy-bentham-vol-2*.

Black Lives Matter. n.d. "About" at *https://blacklivesmatter.com/about/*.

Blackstone, William, 1803/1996. *Blackstone's Commentaries*, vol. II. St. George Tucker, ed. Union, New Jersey: Lawbook Exchange.

Carmines, Edward G. and Robert Huckfeldt. 1992. "Party Politics in the Wake of the Voting Rights Act," in Bernard Grofman and Chandler Davidson, eds.

Controversies in Minority Voting. Washington D.C.: Brookings: 117-134.

Commission of Inquiry into the Black Panthers and Police. 1973. *Search and Destroy.* New York: Metropolitan Applied Research Center.

Dohm, Christian Wilhelm von. 1781/2011. "Concerning the Amelioration of the Civil Status of Jews," excerpt in Mendes-Flohr and Reinharz, pp. 27-34.

Douglass, Frederick. 1854/2016. "The Claims of the Negro Ethnologically Considered," in *The Portable Frederick Douglass,* John Stauffer and Henry Louis Gates, eds. New York: Penguin, pp. 223-247.

_____. 1857. "West India Emancipation Speech." Available at *https://rbscp.lib.rochester.edu/4398*.

Finkelman, Paul. 2017. *Dred Scott v. Sandford: A Brief History with Documents,* second edition. New York: St. Martin's.

Girgis, Sherif, Ryan T. Anderson, and Robert P. George. 2012. *What is Marriage?: Man and Woman: A Defense.* New York: Encounter Books.

Glendon, Mary Ann. 2002. *A World Made New.* New York: Random House.

Gouge, Olympe de. 1791. *Declaration of the Rights of Woman and the Female Citizen.* Available at *https://pages.uoregon.edu/dluebke/301ModernEurope/GougesRightsofWomen.pdf*

Hall, Jacquelyn Dowd. 2005. "The Long Civil Rights Movement and the Political Uses of the Past." *Journal of American History* 91: 1233-1263.

Hanisch, Carol. 1969. "The Personal is Political." Available at http://www.carolhanisch.org/CHwritings/PIP.html.

_____. 1978. "The Liberal Takeover of Women's Liberation" in *Feminist Revolution* , Kathie Sarachild, ed. New York: Random House, pp. 163-167. Online edition available at https://www.redstockings.org/images/stories/CatalogPDFs/FR/31-Feminist-Revolution-The-Liberal-Takeover-of-Womens-Liberation-Carol-Hanisch.pdf.

Haywood, Harry. 1948. *Negro Liberation*. New York: International Publishers.

Herzl. Theodor. 1896/1988. *The Jewish State*, translated by Sylvie d'Avigdor. New York: Dover. Available at https://www.gutenberg.org/files/25282/25282-h/25282-h.htm#I_Introduction.

Honneth, Axel. 2015. *The Idea of Socialism*. Malden, Massachusetts: Polity.

Hurston, Zora Neale. 1955. "Letter to the Editor". *Orlando Sentinel*. August 11. Available at https://teachingamericanhistory.org/library/document/letter-to-the-orlando-sentinel/.

Kilpatrick, James Jackson. 1965. "Must We Repeal the Constitution to Give Negroes the Vote?" *National Review*. April 20: 319-322.

King, Jr., Martin Luther. 1967/2004. "Where do We Go from Here" in *Martin Luther King Jr., Malcolm X, and the Civil Rights Struggle of the 1950's and 1960's*, David Howard-Pitney, ed. New York: Bedford/St. Martin's, pp. 147-157.

_____. 1986. *Testament of Hope: The Essential Writings and Speeches of Martin Luther King, Jr.* James M. Washington, ed. New York: HarperCollins.

Laughlin, Kathleen A. et al. 2010. "Is It Time to Jump Ship? Historians Rethink the Waves Metaphor." *Feminist Formations* 22: 76-135.

Lewis, George. *Massive Resistance: The White Response to the Civil Rights Movement.* London: Hodder Arnold.

Locke, John. 1689/1983. *A Letter Concerning Toleration*, James H. Tully, ed. Indianapolis, Indiana: Hackett Publishing.

_____. 1690/1952. *The Second Treatise of Government*, Thomas P. Peardon ed. Indianapolis, Indiana: Bobbs-Merrill.

Luther, Martin. 1543/1948. T*he Jews and Their Lies.* Los Angeles, California: Christian Nationalist Crusade.

Macedo, Stephen. 1996. "Sexual Morality and the New Natural Law," in R.P. George, ed. *Natural Law, Liberalism, and Morality*, Oxford: Oxford University Press.

Malcolm X. 1964a. "Speech at the Founding Rally of the Organization of African-American Unity." Available at *https://www.blackpast.org/african-american-history/ speeches-african-american-history/1964-malcolm-x- s-speech-founding-rally-organization-afro-american- unity/.*

_____. 1964b. "The Ballot or the Bullet." Available at *http://americanradioworks.publicradio.org/features/ blackspeech/mx.html.*

Marx, Karl. 1843/ 1978. "On the Jewish Question," in *The Marx-Engels Reader*, second edition, Robert Tucker, ed. New York: W.W. Norton, pp. 26-52.

Mendelssohn, Moses. 1783/2011. "Remarks Concerning Michaelis's Response to Dohm," translated by J. Hessing, in Mendes-Flohr and Reinharz, eds. 2011, pp. 40-41.

Mendes-Flohr, Paul and Jehuda Reinharz. 2011. *The Jew in the Modern World: A Documentary History*. New York: Oxford University Press.

Michaelis, Johann David. 1782/2011. "Arguments Against Dohm," translated by L. Sachs, in Mendes-Flohr and Reinharz, eds. 2011, pp. 34-36.

Mill, John Stuart. 1859/2010. "On Liberty," in *On Liberty and Other* Essays. Digireads.com, pp. 113-256.

_____. 1869/2010. "On the Subjection of Women," in *On Liberty and Other* Essays. Digireads.com, pp. 256-318.

Napoleon. 1808/2011. "Decree on the Regulation of Commercial Transactions and Residence of Jews," translated by S.J. Maslin, in Mendes-Flohr and Reinharz, eds. 2011, pp. 161-163.

National Coalition for Women and Girls in Education (NCWGE). 2017. *Title IX at 45*. Washington, D.C. : NCWGE.

Nussbaum, Martha. 2010. "Veiled Threats," *New York Times*, July 11. Available at https://opinionator.blogs.nytimes.com/2010/07/11/veiled-threats/.

Parker, Theodore. 1852. "Of Justice and the Conscience." Available at *http://www.fusw.org/uploads/1/3/0/4/13041662/of-justice-and-the-conscience.pdf*.

Patterson, Orlando. 1982. *Slavery and Social Death*. Cambridge, Massachusetts: Harvard University Press.

Redstockings. 1969. "Redstockings Manifesto." Available at *https://www.redstockings.org/index.php/rs-manifesto*.

Reed, Adolph, Jr. 2016. "How Racial Disparity Does Not Help Make Sense of Patterns of Police Violence." September 16, at *https://nonsite.org/editorial/how-racial-disparity-does-not-help-make-sense-of-patterns-of-police-violence*.

Rosenberg, Gerald N. 1993. *The Hollow Hope*. Chicago: University of Chicago Press.

Sarachild, Kathie. 1978. "The Power of History," in *Feminist Revolution,* Sarachild, ed. New York: Random House, pp. 13-43.

Sieyès, Emmanuel Joseph. 1789/2014. "Reasoned Exposition of the Rights of Man and Citizen," in Oliver W. Lembcke and Florian Weber, eds. *Emmanuel Joseph Sieyès: The Essential Political Writings*. Leiden: Brill.

Traynor, Ian. 2008. " 'I don't hate Muslims. I hate Islam', says Holland's Rising Political Star." *The Guardian*, February 16. Available at *https://www.theguardian.com/world/2008/feb/17/netherlands.islam*.

Treitschke, Heinrich von. 1879. "Our Views." Available at *http://ghdi.ghi-dc.org/sub_document.cfm?document_id=1799*.

Ture, Kwame (Stokley Carmichael) and Charles. V. Hamilton. 1967/1992. *Black Power*. New York: Vintage.

Walker, David. 1829. *Appeal in Four Articles*. Available at https://docsouth.unc.edu/nc/walker/walker.html.

Wecshler, Herbert. 1959. "Toward Neutral Principles of Constitutional Law." *Harvard Law Review 73*: 1-35.

Whitman, James. 2017. *Hitler's American Model.* Princeton, New Jersey: Princeton University Press.

Wilson, Woodrow. 1918. "Fourteen Points Speech." Available at *https://usa.usembassy.de/etexts/democrac/51.htm*.

Wollstonecraft, Mary. 1791/1988. *A Vindication of the Rights of Women.* Carol H. Poston, ed. New York: W.W. Norton.

Further reading

Ackerman, Bruce. 2014. *The Civil Rights Revolution*. Cambridge, Massachusetts: Harvard University Press.

Alexander, Michelle. 2020. *The New Jim Crow*. New York: New Press.

Becker, Lawrence. 2005. "Reciprocity, Justice, and Disability," *Ethics* 116: 9–39.

Branch, Taylor. 2013. *The King Years: Historic Moments in the Civil Rights Movement*. New York: Simon and Schuster.

Brubaker, William Rogers. 1989. "The French Revolution and the Invention of Citizenship," *French Politics, Culture, and Society* 7: 30-49.

Corvino, John and Maggie Gallagher. 2012. *Debating Same-Sex Marriage*. New York: Oxford University Press.

Crenshaw, Kimberlé. 1989/1998. "Demarginalizing the Intersection of Race and Sex: A Black Feminist Critique of Antidiscrimination Doctrine, Feminist Theory and Antiracist Politics." *Feminism and Politics*, A. Phillips, ed. New York: Oxford University Press. pp. 314–343.

Du Bois, W.E.B. 1935 /1998. *Black Reconstruction in America: 1860-1880.* New York: Free Press.

Dubois, Laurent. 2004. *Avengers of the New World: The Story of the Haitian Revolution.* Cambridge, Massachusetts: Harvard University Press.

Epstein, Richard. 1995. *Forbidden Grounds: The Case Against Employment Discrimination Law.* Cambridge, Massachusetts: Harvard University Press.

Evans, Richard J. 1977. *The Feminists.* Beckenham, U.K.: Croom Helm.

Francis, Leslie P. and Anita Silvers, eds. 2000. *Americans with Disabilities.* New York: Routledge.

George, Walter F. et al. 1956. "Declaration of Constitutional Principles" (the "Southern Manifesto"). Available at http://web.utk.edu/~mfitzge1/docs/374/TSM1956.pdf.

Goldfarb, Michael. 2009. *Emancipation: How Liberating Europe's Jews from the Ghetto Led to Revolution and Renaissance.* New York: Simon and Schuster.

Hellman, Deborah and Sophia Moreau, eds. 2013. *Philosophical Foundations of Discrimination Law.* Oxford: Oxford University Press.

James, C.L.R. 1938/1989. *The Black Jacobins*, second ed. revised. New York: Random House.

Joseph, Peniel E. 2006. *Waiting 'Til the Midnight Hour: A Narrative History of Black Power in America*. New York: Holt.

Katz, Jacob. 1971. *Tradition and Crisis: Jewish Society at the End of the Middle Ages*. New York: Schocken.

Kymlicka, Will. 1995. *Multicultural Citizenship*. Oxford: Clarendon Press.

MacKinnon, Catharine. 1988. *Feminism Unmodified*. Cambridge, Massachusetts: Harvard University Press.

McIntosh, Kriston, Emily Moss, Ryan Nunn, and Jay Shambaugh. 2020. "Examining the Black-White Wealth Gap." Available at https://www.brookings.edu/blog/up-front/2020/02/27/examining-the-black-white-wealth-gap/.

Massey and Denton. 1993. *American Apartheid*. Cambridge, Massachusetts: Harvard University Press.

Murray, Pauli, and Mary O. Eastwood. 1965. "Jane Crow and the Law: Sex Discrimination and Title VII." *George Washington Law Review* 34: 232-56.

Newton, Huey. 1966. "The Ten-Point Program." Available at https://www.marxists.org/history/usa/workers/black-panthers/1966/10/15.htm.

Nussbaum, Martha. 2000. *Sex and Social Justice*. New York: Oxford University Press.

Oliver, Melvin and Thomas Shapiro. 2006. *Black Wealth/White Wealth*. New York: Routledge.

Rosselli, Carlo. 1930/1994. *Liberal Socialism*. William McCuaig, trans. and Nadia Urbinati, ed. Princeton, New Jersey: Princeton University Press.

Shelby, Tommie and Brandon M. Terry, eds. 2018. *To Shape a New World: Essays on the Political Philosophy of Martin Luther King, Jr.* Cambridge, Massachusetts: Harvard University Press.

Sinha, Mansha. 2016. *The Slave's Cause: A History of Abolition*. New Haven, Connecticut: Yale University Press.

Silvers, Anita, David Wasserman and Mary B. Mahowald, eds. 1999. *Disability, Difference, Discrimination*. Lanham, Maryland: Rowman and Littlefield.

Sorkin, David. 2019. *Jewish Emancipation*. Princeton, New Jersey: Princeton University Press.

Sunstein, Cass. 1994. "The Anticaste Principle." *Michigan Law Review* 92: 2410–2455.

Vandenhole, Wouter. 2005. *Non-Discrimination and Equality in the View of the UN Human Rights Treaty Bodies*, Oxford: Intersentia.

A Quick Immersion series

For more information, please follow us on Facebook @TibidaboPublishing or visit www.quickimmersions.com